Attracting the Best

How the Military Competes for Information Technology Personnel

JAMES R. HOSEK, MICHAEL G. MATTOCK, C. CHRISTINE FAIR,
JENNIFER KAVANAGH, JENNIFER SHARP, MARK TOTTEN

Supported by the Office of the Secretary of Defense
Approved for public release; distribution unlimited

RAND NATIONAL DEFENSE RESEARCH INSTITUTE

The research described in this report was sponsored by the Office of the Secretary of Defense (OSD). The research was conducted in the RAND National Defense Research Institute, a federally funded research and development center supported by the OSD, the Joint Staff, the unified commands, and the defense agencies under Contract DASW01-01-C-0004.

Library of Congress Cataloging-in-Publication Data

Attracting the best : how the military competes for information technology personnel / James Hosek ... [et al.].
p. cm.
"MG-108."
Includes bibliographical references.
ISBN 0-8330-3550-9 (pbk. : alk. paper)
1. United States—Armed Forces—Recruiting, enlistment, etc. 2. Electronic data processing personnel—Recruiting—United States. I. Hosek, James R.

UB323.A85 2004
355.2'2362—dc22

2003028056

Published 2004 by the RAND Corporation
1700 Main Street, P.O. Box 2138, Santa Monica, CA 90407-2138
1200 South Hayes Street, Arlington, VA 22202-5050
201 North Craig Street, Suite 202, Pittsburgh, PA 15213-1516
RAND URL: http://www.rand.org/
To order RAND documents or to obtain additional information, contact
Distribution Services: Telephone: (310) 451-7002;
Fax: (310) 451-6915; Email: order@rand.org

Preface

In the final years of the 1990s, the private-sector demand for information technology (IT) workers seemed insatiable. IT unemployment was practically nonexistent, pay was high and rising fast, and the Bureau of Labor Statistics had forecast a far larger growth in IT jobs over the next decade than in any other occupational area. Leaders in the national security community began to doubt that the military, intelligence agencies, and public organizations would be able to compete for IT workers in such an increasingly tight labor market. This concern was intensified by the evolving nature of the military services and intelligence agencies and their increasing dependence on information technology. The scramble for IT workers has ceased, but it lasted long enough to jolt state and federal agencies into modifying their personnel policies to attract and keep IT personnel, e.g., through altered job classification systems, increased pay levels, and enhanced professional development opportunities. The IT boom also caused national security planners to question whether future force structures would be vulnerable to shortages of IT personnel.

This report addresses a component of this issue by focusing on the factors affecting the supply of IT personnel to the active duty enlisted force. In brief, the findings point to the conclusion that the IT training opportunities offered by the military can help secure the supply of IT personnel over the long haul. The intended audience of this report is the defense manpower policy research community; Pentagon analysts; congressional staffers; and command, control, communications, and intelligence staff who are interested in the supply of IT personnel.

The report was prepared under the sponsorship of the National Defense Research Institute Advisory Board, with cosponsorship from the Office of the Under Secretary of Defense for Personnel and Readiness and the Office of the Assistant Secretary of Defense for Command, Control, Communications, and Intelligence. It was prepared within the Forces and Resources Policy Center of the RAND Corporation's National Defense Research Institute, a federally funded research and development center sponsored by the Office of the Secretary of Defense, the Joint Staff, the unified commands, and the defense agencies.

Comments are welcome and may be addressed to the Project Leader, James Hosek, james_hosek@rand.org. For more information on RAND's Forces and Resources Policy Center, contact the director, Susan Everingham, susan_everingham@rand.org, 310-393-0411, extension 7654.

The RAND Corporation Quality Assurance Process

Peer review is an integral part of all RAND research projects. Prior to publication, this document, as with all documents in the RAND monograph series, was subject to a quality assurance process to ensure that the research meets several standards, including the following: The problem is well formulated; the research approach is well designed and well executed; the data and assumptions are sound; the findings are useful and advance knowledge; the implications and recommendations follow logically from the findings and are explained thoroughly; the documentation is accurate, understandable, cogent, and temperate in tone; the research demonstrates understanding of related previous studies; and the research is relevant, objective, independent, and balanced. Peer review is conducted by research professionals who were not members of the project team.

RAND routinely reviews and refines its quality assurance process and also conducts periodic external and internal reviews of the quality of its body of work. For additional details regarding the RAND quality assurance process, visit http://www.rand.org/standards/.

Contents

Figures

Tables

Summary

The late-1990s peak in demand for information technology (IT) workers led private firms to respond by offering higher pay, enhanced on-the-job training opportunities, flexible work hours, and support for career development. The economic boom, the rapid growth of information technology as an occupation, and the record low unemployment rates in the private sector created recruiting and retention challenges for the military, which found itself depending more and more on information technology. In fact, during this same period, the military services embarked on initiatives to employ information technology in a host of ways that extended military capability on the battlefield, in intelligence, and in support activities. The services also implemented programs to certify a member's expertise in information technology, e.g., in system administration or in networks.

The convergence of IT trends in the public and private sector intensified the competition between the military and private corporations for IT workers. In addition, the military's efforts to recruit into IT were complicated by several factors. The general increase in civilian wages outpaced the increase in military pay, and civilian wages in IT rose more quickly than in non-IT. Because military pay in IT and non-IT occupations remained similar to each other, the military/civilian wage ratio not only declined overall, but it declined more for service personnel in IT occupations than in non-IT occupations. Furthermore, the budget for enlistment and reenlistment bonuses and educational benefits were low in the mid-1990s, contributing to recruiting difficulties and to retention difficulties in some specialties.

These conditions—burgeoning private-sector demand for IT workers, escalating private-sector pay in IT, growing military dependence on IT, and faltering military recruiting—led to a concern that military capability was vulnerable to a large shortfall in IT personnel. What basis, if any, offered assurance that the supply of IT personnel would be adequate to meet the military's future IT manpower requirements?

In addressing this question, we undertook a number of related tasks. We surveyed literature on managing and compensating IT workers in private firms and in government, conducted field interviews on selected IT occupations in the Army and the Air Force, studied data on military personnel in IT and non-IT occupations, and compared military pay with civilian wages in IT and non-IT occupations. The results of our research led to the preliminary conclusions that not only had the military competed successfully for IT personnel, but that the value and transferability of military IT training had been a key factor in this competition. To gain a more rigorous conceptual understanding of these conclusions, we proceeded to develop a dynamic, stochastic theoretical model of IT personnel supply. The model provides a cohesive framework for exploring a set of factors that affect the enlistment and retention of IT versus non-IT personnel and for absorbing and rationalizing the observations drawn from our surveys and regressions. Taken together, the literature review, field interviews, data analysis, and dynamic model compose an integrative perspective on the issue we set out to study and offer some policy implications for military planners in terms of how to recruit and retain qualified IT personnel. In addition, the insights of this research seem likely to apply to other high-tech occupations in the military that, like IT, offer valuable, transferable training in addition to the opportunity to serve.

The Services Have Been Successful in Attracting and Keeping IT Personnel

Despite obstacles the military faced in recruiting IT personnel and competing with private-sector firms, our research indicates that each service succeeded in recruiting and retaining IT personnel. In fact, we find that compared with non-IT recruits, IT recruits were of higher quality, signed on for somewhat longer terms, had lower attrition, and had similar rates of reenlistment (except in the Army, where IT reenlistment was lower).

IT Training Appears to Be Central to the Attractiveness of Military IT Positions to Potential Recruits

To explain the attractiveness of IT to a potential military recruit, it is necessary to look at the value and transferability of military IT training to civilian jobs. A prospective recruit who is not already in IT will be drawn to the military not only by the challenge of military service, but also by the opportunity to gain IT training, especially considering that many of the IT skills learned in the military can be used in civilian IT jobs. Enlistment incentives, namely, bonuses and educational benefits, can also be used to attract recruits to IT or other specialties. However, we found only minor differences in bonus and benefit usage between IT and non-IT specialties, which suggested that the value of IT training may have reduced the need for higher enlistment incentives in IT.

Our results indicate that military IT training is an important ingredient to the successful fulfillment of IT manpower requirements because of its ability to attract IT personnel. However, it would also seem that as a result of the private-sector value of IT training received in the military, IT military personnel would have a higher incentive to leave the military for civilian jobs with higher wages. This implies that keeping trained IT personnel may be more of a challenge than recruiting IT personnel. Yet while trained IT personnel may have more of an incentive to leave the military, we found that IT reenlistment rates were slightly lower in the Army and the Navy, about the same in the Air Force, and slightly higher in the Marine Corps than non-IT reenlistment rates. Although we expect that reenlistment behaviors were influenced by reenlistment bonus usage and/or bonus amounts, which we found to be higher in IT than in non-IT occupations in several services, we also believe that reenlistment was influenced by the expectation of receiving still further valuable training and career growth opportunities in IT.

Even If Future IT Manning Requirements Change, the Military Should Be Able to Meet Its Needs

The services have long-term visions of future military capabilities and force structures, but, not surprisingly, these visions do not detail manpower requirements. However, the services have a much firmer idea of the weapons systems and doctrinal changes that will come into effect in the near term. These changes typically affect only a portion of the force at any given time. Furthermore, the services have processes to define the manpower requirements for these changes, and the planning cycle is generally long enough to allow manpower supply to adjust. As a result of these established planning cycles, if IT manpower requirements continue to change at a gradual pace, and if military IT training continues to be valued in civilian jobs, there is reason to believe that the services will be able to meet their future IT manpower requirements.

As a caution, large, abrupt increases in IT manpower requirements will decrease this likelihood. Yet it is worth noting that the number and percentage of recruiting slots designated as IT in our study have declined over the past 20 years. The enormous increases in the productivity of information technology may have enabled the military to do more with fewer people, and further, some IT tasks may have been outsourced. Finally, because success in IT recruiting has depended on the value of military IT training in civilian jobs, a softening of the civilian demand for IT workers can only reduce that value and increase the difficulty of recruiting into IT. However, enlistment and reenlistment incentives such as bonuses can help to compensate for such a loss in value.

Acknowledgments

We thank David Gompert, who emphasized the importance of information technology personnel in future national security planning and aided us in securing the initial funding for this project. Our project monitors, Judy Fernandez, Office of the Under Secretary of Defense (Personnel and Readiness), and Joyce France, Office of the Assistant Secretary of Defense (Command, Control, Communications, and Information), helped in all stages of the project, especially at the beginning as the project's scope and direction were set. Susan Everingham, director of the Center for Forces and Resource Policy within the National Security Research Division at RAND, participated in the initial phase of work and provided valuable managerial guidance and research insight over the remainder of the project. We received information and assistance from many Army, Navy, Marine Corps, and Air Force officers and enlisted personnel who took part in field interviews and met with us in the Pentagon; although we do not list them individually, we deeply appreciate their contribution. Judy Fernandez, Chad Shirley of RAND, and Professor of Economics Stephan Mehay at the U.S. Naval Postgraduate School reviewed the report overall, and Jennie Wenger of the Center for Naval Analyses reviewed the theoretical model and simulations. We sincerely thank them for their thorough, constructive reviews, and we have done our best to respond to them. Finally, we thank Kristin Leuschner and Christina Pitcher for their efforts to lend clarity and concision to our writing.

CHAPTER ONE

Introduction and Overview

Information technology (IT) permeates current plans for the ongoing transformation of the military and past experiences in military evolution. In fact, the potent role of IT had already become apparent in World War II, with the emergence of radio communications on the battlefield, the advent of radar and sonar, the use of onboard electromechanical computers for targeting battleship guns, and the use of primitive computers in the decryption analysis at Bletchley Park. In the 1990s, the Army took major strides toward "digitizing" its forces; the Navy networked the logistics of its Pacific fleet with commercially available software; and the Air Force made increasing use of satellite imaging, location, and communications technology. Most recently, IT played a major role in supporting joint service operations in Iraq.

Research in areas such as tank crew performance (Scribner et al., 1986), multichannel radio operation (Winkler and Polich, 1990; Fernandez, 1992), Patriot missile crew performance (Orvis, Childress, and Polich, 1992), ship readiness (Junor and Oi, 1996), and maintenance (Gotz and Stanton, 1986) has shown that the quality and experience of personnel make a large difference in how effectively weapons systems are operated and maintained and, therefore, in military capability and readiness. It seems likely that this observation can be extended to IT occupations and personnel. That is, the effectiveness of military systems that depend on IT will in turn depend on the quality and experience of personnel in IT, and conversely, reductions in quality and experience of IT personnel, or outright shortfalls in the supply of IT personnel, can jeopardize military capability and readiness.

Given the growing role of IT and the dependence of IT system performance on IT personnel, the National Defense Research Institute (NDRI) Advisory Board asked the RAND Corporation to assess whether the supply of IT personnel would be adequate to meet emerging IT manpower requirements. This request suggested structuring a study that would review the long-term IT manpower requirements, analyze the supply of IT personnel, and determine whether there was likely to be a gap between supply and requirements. Although we began by looking into long-term requirements, we learned that while the services have long-term visions of force structures, they do not detail long-term manpower requirements. However, we also learned (as discussed in Chapter Three) that the services have reasonably specific knowledge of system changes to be implemented in the near term. These changes affect only a part of the force at any time and in this sense have an evolutionary, not discontinuous, affect on manpower requirements. Furthermore, the cycle of near-term changes has generally been long enough to allow the development of training and the design of career tracks to adapt to the emerging manpower requirements. These findings led us to orient the research around IT personnel supply. We wanted to gain firsthand knowledge of how the services and other organizations were managing IT occupations, determine whether the supply of IT personnel had lapsed during the late-1990s boom, and identify factors affecting IT recruiting and retention.

Also, as we mapped out the scope of our inquiry, we decided to focus on the supply of enlisted personnel. We undertook a review of the literature, conducted fieldwork, and reviewed data on IT personnel with regard to quality, term length, attrition, and reenlistment. In addition, we studied civilian wages in IT and non-IT occupations and compared those wages to military pay. Finally, we developed a theoretical model of the supply and retention of IT personnel to further support our argument and to provide additional insight into the issue at hand. Similar research could be done on officers and Department of Defense (DoD) civilians, but it was beyond the scope of the present work.

Overview of Findings

The Literature Emphasizes the Impact of IT on the Economy and the Workforce but Is Ambiguous on the Question of a Potential Shortage of IT Workers

Academic research, the popular press, and congressional testimony all provided insights into the nature and development of IT within the private and public sectors (Chapter Two). Having played a more modest role in the 1980s, IT emerged as a major contributor to economic expansion in the 1990s. Also, IT may have contributed to the increase in wage variance among workers by acting as a substitute for menial-task workers, keeping their wages down, and a complement for workers in high-cognition tasks, pushing their wages up. IT transformed the ways goods and services were produced and distributed, thereby destroying some jobs and creating others.

The popular press touted private-sector IT positions for their access to the newest hardware and software, emphasis on continuing training, flexible work schedules, and staunch employer support for building one's career. Despite this rosy image, we found no random, representative surveys of these "ideal" practices, and it is unclear how prevalent they were. The popular press also mentioned a negative facet of private-sector practice—flexible work schedules were often accompanied by long hours of work.

Of particular interest to this research, the literature records conflicting views on the potential for a massive national shortage in IT workers. On the one hand, there were widespread perceptions in the 1990s that such a shortage was imminent because of the projected growth in demand for IT workers and the low numbers of IT graduates being produced by colleges and universities. For example, the Bureau of Labor Statistics forecasted an increase of over one million IT jobs from 1994 to 2005. On the other hand, analysts argued that adjustments would mitigate the shortage and allow IT manning requirements to be met. For example, workers from non-IT backgrounds can be trained into IT, as has often been the case in the past. Also, organizations can increase pay and redesign jobs in IT to make them more attractive, and IT positions and requirements can be simplified and adapted so that they fit the skills of the extant workforce instead of creating a demand for "IT" workers.

Interviews Shed Light on the Challenges Facing the Military in Recruiting, Training, and Developing the IT Workforce

To extend the findings from our literature review to the armed services, we conducted fieldwork, in the form of interviews, on the management of IT occupations in the Army and the Air Force. These interviews, which are discussed in Chapter Three, shed light on the challenges facing the military services in their attempts to attract, train, and develop a sizable and highly skilled IT workforce—as well as the procedures and capabilities in place to address these challenges.

From the viewpoint of the people we interviewed, retention was the foremost challenge. The loss of high-tech military personnel to industry caused problems throughout the force and had a negative effect on readiness and capability. For example, some positions went unfilled, and sometimes positions were filled by accelerating the promotion of members who did not yet have the skills and experience needed to be good leaders and mentors to train junior personnel. Interviewees also feared that course instructors supplied by contractors would "poach" military members, particularly if reenlistment bonuses were low or absent.

The lack of financial incentives to obtain additional education and training was a related problem. Military members received no reward, e.g., no special pay, for learning a new skill or completing a course. Some interviewees cited this as a deterrent to entering IT and an obstacle to reenlistment. However, others said military training was valuable in civilian jobs and should be viewed as a form of deferred compensation. By the latter view, the incentive to remain in the military depends on the continued provision of valuable training.

Other problems relating to IT occupations included the lengthy delays in obtaining top-secret clearances, thus preventing members who had trained for intelligence positions from being assigned to them, and the high operational tempo and frequency of deployment found in certain intelligence specialties.

With respect to future manpower requirements, the Army and the Air Force have processes in place to anticipate future manning and training requirements. The processes are geared to the pace at which resource decisions are made, which in the case of new systems or hardware often means a cycle of planning and procurement four years or longer. It is our impression that the processes have been responsive to speedups in the planning/procurement cycle. However, although the interviews offered helpful information, a full assessment of the optimality and flexibility of the requirement determination process would need a separate analysis.

Analysis of Data Indicates High Quality of IT Recruits, Lengthier Terms, and Lower Attrition

The economic conditions in the late 1990s, the glowing description of IT employment conditions appearing in the popular press, the projections for a massive shortfall in IT workers in the future, and the weakening state of military recruiting and retention were all reasons to expect an acute supply problem in military IT. But the data on IT recruit quality, term length, and attrition told a different story (Chapter Four). From the mid-1990s through 2001, recruit quality was higher in IT than in non-IT occupations. Furthermore, although choice of contract length does not rest entirely with the recruit and is controlled partially by the services' decisions about how to structure their recruiting quotas, IT recruits were more likely than non-IT recruits to have a longer initial term (of five or six years) and to stay to complete their term. Since IT recruits were of higher quality, it was not surprising, based on past studies, to find higher term completion in IT than in non-IT. But even holding quality constant, term completion was higher in IT than in non-IT. Also, the use of enlistment bonuses was little different in IT than in non-IT, although our data on bonuses were limited.

The reenlistment picture was mixed. Reenlistment was lower in IT than in non-IT in the Army and the Navy, roughly the same in the Air Force, and higher in IT than in non-IT in the Marine Corps. These differences probably trace to differences in the use of reenlistment bonuses and in the perceived value of a continued career in IT versus non-IT. Wider use of bonuses, higher bonus amounts, and a high value of additional training and experience in IT would increase the retention rate in IT and perhaps make it higher than the rate in non-IT.

Our wage analysis (Chapter Five) found civilian wages to be considerably higher in IT than in non-IT, as we had expected. To compare military pay to civilian wages, we used regular military compensation (RMC), which is the sum of basic pay, housing and subsistence allowances, and the federal tax advantage deriving from the allowances not being taxed. RMC on average accounts for over 90 percent of a member's take-home pay. RMC lay near the 70th percentile of civilian wages for non-IT male workers with some college, but near the 50th percentile of wages for IT male workers with some college. By implication, the military/civilian pay ratio was lower in IT than in non-IT. (Comparisons for other education levels and for women are also given in Chapter Five.) Because lower relative pay was another reason to expect supply problems in IT, the strong results in IT recruiting and similar levels of reenlistment for IT and non-IT pointed to the conclusion that the military offers in-kind value in the IT field in the form of training and experience.

Conclusions: Restructuring IT Careers

The evidence indicates that IT training and experience are a compensating differential that helps support the military's ability to compete for IT recruits, despite the higher pay and amenities in civilian IT jobs. IT training and experience, augmented by enlistment bonuses and educational benefits as needed, seem sufficient to ensure an adequate flow of new recruits into IT. For the same reasons, the retention of IT personnel beyond the first term will depend on the value of further military IT training and experience, and of course on reenlistment incentives. If IT manpower requirements continue to evolve gradually, as they have for two decades, and if military IT training remains valuable in civilian jobs, we expect the military to be able to meet its future IT manpower requirements.

However, a sharp increase in military IT manpower requirements or the recurrence of a dot-com bubble could create difficulties. Depending on the likelihood of these occurrences, the military could develop hedging strategies such as maintaining an "excess" supply of trained IT personnel at certain grade-experience levels. Furthermore, if the military wants more flexibility in managing IT personnel—to have more varied career lengths, longer time in assignments, or longer time in certain ranks—IT careers and compensation will need to be restructured. The need for restructuring will depend on the value to the member of remaining in the military; if the member continues to gain valuable, transferable skills, the compensating differential mechanism will continue to operate.

Organization of This Report

We describe the results of our literature review in Chapter Two, and we discuss the results of interviews with Army and Air Force personnel in Chapter Three. Chapter Four compares enlisted personnel flows in IT occupations with those in non-IT occupations, while Chapter Five analyzes civilian wages in IT and non-IT and compares them with military pay. In Chapter Six, we discuss a model that supports the validity of our argument and provides information on the mechanisms that affect IT recruitment and retention. Finally, Chapter Seven offers our conclusion and suggestions for future research on this topic. The appendixes contain a listing of military and civilian IT occupations used in this report, regressions on the personnel flows, wage comparisons for men and women with more than four years of college, and the technical development of the model in Chapter Six.

CHAPTER TWO

Issues and Practices in Managing IT Occupations: Views from the Literature

In this chapter, we examine discussions of IT occupations as found in existing academic literature, the popular press, and congressional testimony. We begin with a brief background section, in which we define what is included within the topic of "IT occupations," and present an overview of some of the IT themes found in the literature.

We then shift our focus more specifically to the subject of IT worker management and compensation in the public and private sectors. One of the key issues discussed in relation to both sectors is a possible shortage of IT workers. Our literature review provides a framework for subsequent chapters, in which we present the results of interviews and data analysis regarding the characteristics and incentives of IT workers in the military.

Background: The Scope and Impact of IT Occupations

IT has been described as a "general-purpose technology" because it is adaptable to many uses and arguably of central importance to economic growth.[1] Because of the remarkable technological progress in IT, its adaptation to military and nonmilitary uses is an ongoing and comparatively rapidly evolving process.

What Is an IT Occupation?

To examine the supply of IT workers within the military, we need first to define exactly what is meant by the term "IT occupation." This task is not as simple as it might seem. In recent years, the development, application, and support of IT have become part of all sorts of traditional occupations. When attempting to single out IT occupations, researchers have typically focused on such positions as computer scientists (chip designers and systems architects), systems administrators, systems engineers, and programmers. But ambiguity emerges, for example, when considering workers engaged in hardware and software manufacturing and distribution functions, researchers and other professionals who rely heavily on computers and digital communication, and IT vocational education instructors. All these jobs are related to IT, but should all be classified as "IT positions"? The issue becomes more complicated when we consider the broad expanse of workers who might use some form of IT in their jobs, e.g., repairmen, deliverymen, retail clerks, secretaries, teachers, and so forth.

The literature includes several attempts to define the characteristics of an IT occupation. For example, a National Research Council report distinguishes between *IT workers* and

[1] Bresnahan and Trajtenberg, 1995.

IT-enabled workers; the distinction depends on whether IT knowledge or another domain of knowledge is more important to the value created by the job (National Research Council, 1993). According to this framework, IT workers depend most heavily on IT knowledge and skills to accomplish their objectives, while IT-enabled workers use IT in peripheral capacities to complement other skills that are more essential to the successful completion of their jobs.[2]

However, because IT is increasingly pervasive, a growing proportion of the nation's workers can be considered IT enabled. IT-based communications, reporting, tracking, recordkeeping, bookkeeping, and so forth are commonplace, and as the trend continues it will be no more useful to describe a worker as IT enabled than to describe the worker as electricity enabled. This shortcoming of the above distinction suggests the need for a more nuanced description of IT occupations.

A study by the Computing Research Association designates four categories of IT workers: conceptualizers, developers, modifiers/extenders, and supporters/tenders (see Table 2.1).

Examining the columns in Table 2.1 from left to right, we see that IT occupations can have aspects of both a profession and a trade.

> A trade is a skilled occupation, such as plumbing or carpentry, where training is most likely to occur through an apprenticeship. A profession, such as law or medicine, requires higher education, intellectual problem-solving skills, and certification exams that ensure everyone in the field is familiar with a common body of knowledge (Jacobs, 1998).

Conceptualizers, developers, and modifier/extenders tend more to the professional end of the spectrum in that they involve varying degrees of advanced skills and managerial ability, while supporter/tender occupations might be considered more like trades.

Table 2.1
Categories of Information Technology Workers

Conceptualizers	Developers	Modifiers/Extenders	Supporters/Tenders
Entrepreneur	System designer	Maintenance programmer	System consultant
Product designer	Programmer	Programmer	Customer support specialist
Research engineer	Software engineer	Software engineer	Help desk specialist
Systems analyst	Tester	Computer engineer	Hardware maintenance specialist
Computer science researcher	Computer engineer	Database administrator	Network installer
Requirements analyst	Microprocessor designer		Network administrator
System architect	Chip designer		

SOURCE: Computing Research Association, Intersociety Study Group on Information Technology Workers, April 1999, cited in Freeman and Asprey, 1999, p. 33.

[2] To apply this distinction to the Army, an example of an IT worker would be an MOS 74B information systems operator-analyst, whose "duties involve operating and maintaining information systems, personal computers, network servers, and associated devices." See McHugh, 1998. An example of an IT-enabled worker would be the MOS 92A automated logistical specialist, who works with "state-of-the-art automated systems for ordering, distributing and storing supplies." See Tice, 1998.

The distinction between professional and trade IT occupations corresponds approximately to a classification scheme presented in a recent DoD study group, which distinguished between IT occupations for enlisted and officer personnel (U.S. Office of the Secretary of Defense, 1999). During the 1990s, for the Army, designated IT occupations for enlisted personnel included information systems operator-analyst (74B), record telecommunications operator-maintainer (74C), telecommunications computer operator-maintainer (74G), information systems operator-maintainer (74Z), Army warrant officer: network management technician (250N), and data processing technician (251A). These occupations are similar to those listed in the supporter/tender column above. Designated IT occupations for Army officers included signal, general (25A), and systems automation management (53A). These occupations touch on the categories of conceptualizer, developer, and modifier/extender.

In this report, we use a three-part distinction with reference to IT occupations. "IT-core" occupations are those designated as information technology or information assurance occupations in the Pentagon's IA (information assurance)/IT report (U.S. Office of the Secretary of Defense, 1999). The second category, "IT-related" occupations, includes occupations that rely extensively on IT in duty performance. There are no formal measures for determining what is "IT related," so in defining this category, we have used our best judgment in identifying those occupations that on the surface are very reliant on IT. Such occupations include detection, surveillance, control, and intelligence functions. The third category, "non-IT," includes those occupations that are less reliant on IT, even though many of these occupations may involve the use of IT in some capacity. Table 2.2 illustrates the distinctions among these three categories.

The evolution of the rangefinder in tanks provides an example of the use of IT within non-IT occupations, as was noted above. Over a course of decades, the rangefinder progressed from mechanical to laser to computer-aided laser and, as a result, became much easier for personnel to operate. Army Research Institute psychologists who were assigned to Fort Knox simplified the use of the rangefinder through a systematic, iterated analysis. As discussed by Davis and Wessel (1999),

Table 2.2
IT-Core, IT-Related, and Examples of Other (Non-IT) Military Occupations

IT Core	IT Related	Examples of Non-IT
Information system operator	Navigator	Tracked vehicle maintenance
Telecommunication computer maintainer	Radar, sonar operator	Missile mechanic
Network analyst	Surveillance	Construction
Small computer system specialist	Fire control	Aircraft engine maintenance
Information management	Missile guidance control	Supply administration
Radio communication systems	Electronic countermeasures	Nuclear, biological, chemical warfare
Automated data processing repair	Operational intelligence	Medical, dental
	Mapping	Language interpretation
	Auditing	Security guard
	Precision equipment	Infantry, armor, artillery
		Air crew

> In the 1970s, the Army finally replaced the mechanical rangefinder in the Patton with a laser device. But the problem was, it took an M60 Patton crew twenty-three steps to turn on the finicky laser. In the 1980s, the M1 Abrams was outfitted with a new laser rangefinder, which took just three steps: turn on, point, and click a button to get distance readings. The Army discovered that the simplicity of the M1's laser rangefinder, and other new systems, equalized the skill of gunners, regardless of their education and native talents . . . . 'Any dummy could operate the M1,' explains Lon E. Maggart, the blunt former commanding general of Fort Knox, the Army's armored vehicle training center. 'Your lowest-level soldier could operate this [M1] tank more efficiently than higher-level soldiers on old tanks. The Army made this tank so sophisticated that you just had to push a button.'[3]

The M1A2 succeeded the M1 and M1A1. Introduced in 1992, it has greater lethality and was engineered so that its complex systems "were simplified for use by ordinary Americans who receive little training" (Davis and Wessel, 1999, p. 25).

As this example suggests, the availability of IT means in many cases that formerly complex tasks (operating the M1) can now be performed by personnel with relatively low levels of IT skills and/or training (e.g., the ability to "push a button").

What Effect Has IT Had on the Economy?

IT is important in part because of its positive impact on the economy. For years, the opposite was felt to be the case: Economists found little evidence that IT had much impact on economic growth. As Jorgenson noted, Nobelist Robert Solow lamented that "we see computers everywhere but in the productivity statistics," an observation that came to be known as the Solow Paradox (Jorgenson, 2001; Solow, 1987). Recent research of Jorgenson and his colleagues, however, thoroughly documents the major role IT has played in U.S. economic growth. Most important, Jorgenson emphasizes the enormous price reductions that have accompanied the technological advance of IT. "Between 1974 and 1996 prices of memory chips *decreased* by a factor of 27,270 times or at 40.9 percent per year, while the implicit deflator for the gross domestic product (GDP) *increased* by almost 2.7 times or 4.6 percent per year!" Prices for logic chips decreased even faster (Jorgenson, 2001, p. 3).

Furthermore, following Bresnahan, research has found substantial technological opportunity for further improvement of IT, a feature that links IT closely to economic growth cycles (Bresnahan, undated). As a general-purpose technology, IT has an extremely wide variety of applications that support activities and advances in numerous other areas. Advances in IT facilitate *innovations* ("shift the innovation frontier") rather than directly shifting the production frontier, and these innovations foster the coinvention of other applications. Expansion of the markets for these applications increases the demand for IT, which creates a dynamic feedback loop that raises the return for further innovation in IT. The transforming nature of IT through computing and telecommunications coupled with its ample opportunity for further technological improvement and its fast pace of advance have been key drivers of the revolution in military affairs.

The impact of IT on economic growth took a long time—from the 1970s to the 1990s—to become evident. Recent research on this topic provides some explanations for this phenomenon:

---

[3] The excerpt appears as: "Making It Simple: How Technology Will Make Life Better for Less Skilled Workers," *Army Times*, May 18, 1998, pp. 24–25.

- Technological breakthroughs diffuse slowly because of "high learning costs associated with implementing the new technology" and because "part of this learning is social in that one draws lessons from others' experience." Therefore, a firm or individual has an incentive to delay in adapting in order to capitalize on the learning (trial-and-error efforts) of others (Ifo Institute for Economic Research, 2002).
- The high learning costs might actually cause a decrease in the measured rate of productivity as workers divert effort from production to learning (Greenwood and Yorukoglu, 1997).

What Effect Has IT Had on Wages?

The expansion of IT also appears to have been a key factor influencing both the relatively rapid growth of the wages of college-educated workers throughout the 1980s and into the early 1990s as well as an increase in wage dispersion. Economists have suggested two theoretical explanations for these trends. According to one theory, IT as a factor of production is more complementary with high-skilled labor than with low-skilled labor. The decline in the price of IT led to greater use of IT and induced greater demand for high-skilled labor than for low-skilled labor. Autor, Levy, and Murnane (2001), treating jobs in terms of the tasks they require rather than the educational credentials of those who hold the jobs, have argued that IT "substitutes for a limited and well-defined set of human activities, those involving routine (repetitive) cognitive and manual tasks," and "complements activities involving nonroutine problem-solving and interactive tasks." In commenting on the Autor, Levy, and Murnane work, the Ifo Institute for Economic Research noted that they

> found a high correlation between computerization at the industry level and a shift in the composition of labor input away from routine tasks in favor of nonroutine cognitive tasks. This is direct evidence that computers substitute for tasks performed by low-skilled workers and are complementary with tasks performed by highly educated workers (Ifo Institute for Economic Research, 2002, p. 62).

In related work, Bresnahan further explored the impact of IT on wage distribution, theorizing that IT had caused the "substitution of machine decision making for human decision making in low- and medium-skilled white collar work," but had "not been substitutable for high levels of human cognitive skill in highly-rewarded tasks and occupations" (Bresnahan, 1997). He added that IT had also increased the demand for highly skilled workers by causing changes in the "organization of production at the firm, industry, and even multi-industry level." Finally he noted that "these organizational changes increase the demand for many skills, not just the cognitive ones learned in school," e.g., interpersonal and management skills, autonomy, and judgment.

Synthesizing these complementary arguments on the effect of IT on the wage distribution, it is possible to conclude that since workers might be considered to bring bundles of different skills to their jobs, the IT-driven change in the price of specific skills is responsible for the increase in the dispersion of wages.

IT Workers in the Private Sector

We now look more closely at discussions of IT workers from the private sector. We will first consider discussions of private-sector IT workers in the popular press, and we will then focus on two broad themes often raised in IT-related literature: the issue of a potential shortage of IT personnel and the issue of training and development opportunities in IT occupations.

Views from the Popular Press

Much of the available literature concerning private-sector IT employees comes from the popular press, e.g., newspapers and trade magazines. In addition, this information comes in the form of advice or "tips" rather than data analysis. For example, the May 6, 2002, issue of *Computerworld* offers suggestions to employers on how to manage and motivate IT workers so as to maximize their potential contribution. Themes from the table of contents convey the flavor of such advice:

- IT workers want an employer that can help them be a partner in their career goals.
- To keep workers motivated and loyal, the best employers give them access to hot projects that help advance their careers and stretch their skills.
- The best employers offer access to hot technology and deliver top-drawer training.
- These employers put balance in work and home life. The option to telecommute and a flexible work schedule top the list of low-cost benefits.
- The employers create diversity in culture and ideas.
- To retain top IT workers, the best employers offer more than good jobs—they help build exciting careers.

Although *Computerworld's* suggestions are attractive at face value, they are observations based only on interviews and anecdotes. They are not accompanied by specifics on how to implement such changes and on the cost and benefit to the organization of doing so.

Nonetheless, it is not difficult to find real-world examples that reflect the recommendations. Often such examples have been used in the popular press to illustrate that the *public* sector is falling behind the private sector in attracting and managing IT employees. For instance, an article in the *Los Angeles Times* reported that, "since the government lacks workers with the latest training, its systems tend to be behind the curve. And because the technology is outdated, the work is less attractive to younger computer professionals who put a high priority on keeping their skills current." The article also cites the example of Dwayne Williams, 28, a specialist in network security, formerly with the Air Force, who left the military seeking not only more current technology but also "independence on the job, greater control of his work, and higher compensation" (Shogren , 1999).

While the popular literature often presents private-sector IT workers in a positive light, some stories have described areas of employee dissatisfaction. As one example, an online survey conducted by *Computerworld* in September and October of 1998 reveals that even as the dot-com boom built to its peak, many IT workers were dissatisfied with their salaries. Looking more closely at the issue of higher pay and compensation, a 1998 survey by the American Electronics Association (www.aeanet.org), covering more than 100 smaller high-tech companies with fewer than 500 employees, indicated that increases in pay typically took the form of a combination of higher salaries and higher specific pays, such as retention bonuses (including a skill premium pay), hiring bonuses, and project completion bonuses.

Also, although the salaries of IT workers were higher than those of workers in the non-IT sector, many IT employees also worked more than 40 hours per week, so their higher salaries were in part payment for a longer work week. Many workers reportedly would have preferred a reduced workload and more flexible schedules to higher pay. Finally, most workers were concerned about keeping pace with new IT technology. Although the majority of IT employees responding in the survey had access to the latest hardware and software, they wanted more formal training with accreditation.

Our research also revealed frequent job changes among IT personnel. During the boom, the average stay at a job was 18–24 months. "In certain industries, involving high technology, long periods with the same employer may indicate outdated skills or even a lack of ambition" ("Job-Hopping," 1998). High-level IT skills were in such demand that, according to one survey, four out of five chief information officers would consider becoming an IT consultant if they were out of work. The high demand for IT workers was being driven by the thriving national economy, the burgeoning exploration of the Internet as a basis for business and new business models, and the need to fix year 2000 problems in legacy software. Year 2000 problems increased the demand for older programmers who knew COBOL, and Internet applications fed the demand for young programmers, graphic designers, web page designers, and network installers.

An IT Worker Shortage?

A frequently discussed issue in IT-related literature is the possibility of an IT worker shortage in the near future. Views differ in terms of whether a shortage is actually looming, and the evidence cited in support of either side is sometimes lacking in important ways. For example, a 1999 study issued by the Computing Research Association, an organization representing research scientists, concluded that the "preponderance of evidence suggests that there is a shortage of IT workers, or at least a tight labor market."[4] The study also concluded that the increase in the number of H1B visas—which was temporary and corresponded to IT industry efforts to attract and bring in foreign, specifically Indian, programmers—would not be sufficient to satisfy the long-term growing demand for IT workers. Despite these findings, the study acknowledged the difficulty of determining whether a shortage existed; this was so in part because IT workers come from diverse occupations, and also because available data on supply and demand were out of date and inadequate to detect a shortage directly. Because of these data problems, the study relied on indirect information, e.g., the number of bachelor degrees awarded in computer science, the number of IT training certificates completed, estimates of the growth in IT salaries, and anecdote.

The Bureau of Labor Statistics (BLS) released data that supports the prediction of an IT worker shortage. Its report (Silvestri, 1997) estimated that, between 1994 and 2005, more

---

[4] Freeman and Aspray, 1999, p. 9. This report was triggered by earlier reports by the Information Technology Association of America (ITAA), a trade association of over 11,000 firms, and a report by the Department of Commerce (DoC). The ITAA reports, released in 1997 and 1998 and based on surveys of its member firms, and the DoC report concluded that there was a large shortage of IT workers. The General Accounting Office criticized this conclusion, arguing that the ITAA and DoC studies were flawed because they had not appreciated the difference between a tight labor market and a persistent shortage, and they had downplayed the role of retraining incumbent workers to meet the growing demand for IT skills. See ITAA, 1997, 1998; U.S. Department of Commerce, 1997; U.S. General Accounting Office, 1998.

than a million new computer scientists and engineers, systems analysts, and computer programmers would be needed in the United States. Based on its research, the BLS predicted that the private-sector demand for IT workers would grow more rapidly than job growth overall and that IT workforce salaries would grow more rapidly than the national average as long as the shortage of IT workers persisted.

The opposite hypothesis, that an IT labor shortage was not likely in the near future, was offered in congressional testimony. Indeed, economist Robert Lerman (1998), during his statement before the House Committee on Education and the Workforce, Subcommittee on Oversight and Investigations, contested the notion that IT workers were, or would be, in short supply. He argued that the data purportedly showing a large number of IT job vacancies were not a good indicator of a shortage of IT workers. Vacancy data reflect the current number of open positions; vacancies exist even in a well-functioning labor market with a market-clearing wage. Moreover, he emphasized that the potential pool of IT workers is large since IT workers come from many backgrounds. He illustrated this point with data on college graduates:

> Among the 1992–93 cohort of college graduates, only one-third with jobs in computer science or programming jobs had degrees in computer science or information science. Nearly as large a share came from majors in business management (28 percent). Students with engineering degrees accounted for 12 percent of new graduates working in IT fields.

Other sciences, social sciences, humanities, education, and other fields accounted for the remainder (27 percent).

Contrary to the drumbeat of the popular press and the growing conventional wisdom at that time about the impending crisis in IT worker supply, Lerman found that the projected increase in the supply of college-graduate IT workers would likely meet the large increase in the demand for IT workers forecasted by the Bureau of Labor Statistics. As Table 2.3 shows, he estimated an average annual growth in jobs for operations researchers, programmers, systems analysts, computer engineers, and database administrators of 117,000,

Table 2.3
Projected Annual Growth in Supply and Demand of IT Workers

Projected Supply[a]		Projected Demand[b]	
College Major	Number (thousands)	Occupation	Number (thousands)
Computer and information sciences	57	Operations researcher and programmer	16.9
Engineering	9	Systems analyst	52
Business majors	17.6	Computer engineer	23.5
Other majors	34.2	Database administrator	24.9
Total	117.8	Total	117.3

SOURCE: Lerman, 1998, Chart 5.
[a] Annual growth in college graduates entering IT.
[b] Annual growth in jobs for IT workers, 1996–2006.

based on the Bureau of Labor Statistics estimates. He also predicted an increase in supply from the outflow of college graduates, assuming the graduates followed the same pattern of occupational choice as found for the 1992-93 cohort of college graduates. His supply estimate happens to be virtually equal to his demand estimate, though his method of projecting supply was completely independent of the BLS forecast of demand. Yet even if the demand and supply estimates were not so close, his work would still make the point that the anticipated supply can be expected to satisfy much of the growth in demand. Given that so many non–computer science majors entered IT, it appears as though many college graduates, regardless of their major, responded to job opportunities in IT, and employers who sought IT workers were willing to hire bright people and train them on the job.

Development and Training of IT Workers

The development and training of IT workers is another frequently discussed topic in the literature. Given the speed of IT development and evolution, IT training has become an important issue for employees and employers alike. During the 1990s, employers responded to the demands of a constantly changing IT environment in several ways: strengthening their in-house training and skill development programs, keeping compensation and benefits competitive with the market, and using contractors for short-term demands. Training and development opportunities became part of the overall compensation package offered to IT workers. One type of skill development program might attract college graduates through internships during college summers and rotational, experience-building programs on the job. Another type of program might focus on retraining long-time employees who were skilled, capable, and willing to stay with the organization.

During the 1990s, employee demand for IT training was fueled by the desire to stay current with IT technology. This led IT workers to prize firms that provided access to new technology, offered training opportunities, and generated opportunities to apply or extend the new technology in the business environment. At the same time, employers were able to benefit from employees' ever-increasing skill sets.[5]

IT itself—in the form of new web sites—facilitated employer and employee searches for information about training, job opportunities, and compensation. For example, the Department of Commerce created a web site containing information on IT training programs. The Technology Administration site (www.ta.doc.gov) contained profiles of over 170 systems development programs, including academic and commercial programs, internships, recruitment opportunities, retraining programs, opportunities for the disadvantaged, and programs for teacher development. JobSmart (www.jobsmart.org) provided links to salary surveys for many professions, as did *InformationWeek's* web site (www.informationweek.com/career/default.html) for IT salary comparisons. The user entered his or her job title and the site returned salary information for people in the same region, same industry, or same level of experience. The computer consultant resource page at Realrates (www.realrates.com) let a user compare his or her salary with those of others who knew the same programming languages. The Department of Labor's (www.dol.gov) online job bank had a section devoted to IT positions. The site also included America's Job Bank (AJB), begun in 1995. Employers

[5] The training program of Texas Instruments provides a good example of the types of training programs developed and offered by large corporations. A large number of training courses are offered online (see www.ti-training.com/courses/, last accessed September 2003).

could use AJB to list job openings and review resumes, and job seekers could search for jobs by zip code.

Private contractors capitalized on the high demand for sophisticated training by designing more accessible training programs and certification procedures. For example, Microsoft created Skills 2000, an initiative with three tiers. Tier 1 used job fairs and Monster Board, a job market web site. Tier 2 offered half-price training sessions on Saturdays to keep information systems professionals up to date in Microsoft technology. Tier 3 offered free technical training to academic instructors at high schools, colleges, and universities. Successful students received a certificate as a "Microsoft Certified Professional." The Skills 2000 web site contained an information technology aptitude tool to help applicants determine their potential in eight career categories: database administration, information systems operator/analyst, interactive digital media specialist, network specialist, programmer/analyst, software engineer, technical support representative, and technical writer.

However, research also showed that the constant flow of new IT placed a strain on IT personnel and managers and had some negative effect on IT projects. For example, project failures and budget overruns became common. In one survey, over two-thirds of IT directors reported having had a major IT project failure, and the risk of failure resulted in increased stress that affected personal lives, sometimes leading to breakdowns and depression (Mansell-Lewis, 1998).

As indicated by this review, the expansion of IT in the private sector has brought great benefits to employers and employees, but it has not occurred without costs on both sides. While private-sector IT positions were often compared favorably to their government counterparts in the popular press, a closer analysis of the literature revealed areas of job dissatisfaction among private-sector IT employees as well as concerns among employers about their ability to maintain a sufficient supply of IT workers and the cost of doing so (in terms of compensation and other benefits, such as professional development).

IT Manpower in the Federal Government

Our review of IT-related literature revealed a concern among federal government employers regarding the potential for an IT personnel shortage in military and intelligence agencies. In fact, the House Subcommittee on Technology and Procurement Policy held hearings on what it envisioned as a growing crisis in the federal IT and acquisition workforce. The October 4, 2001, hearing was held to discuss proposed legislation for the recruitment, management, and compensation of federal IT and acquisition workers. Congressional reports on the hearing provide a rich source of information regarding views in the federal government on IT manpower and other personnel issues.

Many of those present at the hearing described their concerns about an impending shortage of IT workers. The chairman of the committee, Rep. Tom Davis of Virginia, anticipated pressure on the IT workforce from three sources: an expected large number of IT retirements over the current decade, a growing demand within government for IT workers, and a continuing growth in demand for IT workers in the private sector. Davis stated that the government would need an additional 16,000 IT hires in 2001 and the private sector would have 425,000 unfilled IT positions.[6] Davis (2001) went on to state that whereas IT held the promise of significant gains in providing government services cost-effectively, the current federal personnel management system was simply not up to the task:

> Unfortunately, the current human resources management system for the vast majority of federal employees in the General Schedules system is dominated by a "one-size-fits-all" philosophy. It is built upon 19th century principles of centralized policy development, selection from rigidly numbered lists of candidates, and uniform pay scales that cannot respond to the different roles, missions and needs of the nearly 100 independent agencies.

Attendees at the meeting went so far as to propose new legislation aimed at addressing and potentially preventing the predicted shortfall by improving the recruitment and retention of IT personnel. The proposed legislation had three main emphases:

- Create a market-based, pay-for-performance system with broad pay bands. "In practice, this would entail broadening the GS 5–15 pay grades into 4 bands. Managers in each agency would be given the authority to set salaries within the bands to correspond with an individual's work performance" (*Federal Acquisition Report*, 2001).
- Add flexibility to recruiting by using excepted service, noncareer appointments that would lead to much faster hiring than under traditional career and career-conditional appointments.
- Encourage the development of additional benefits, e.g., better training and educational opportunities (*Federal Acquisition Report*, 2001).[7]

The General Accounting Office (GAO), which also offered testimony, discussed the assessments of IT human capital management it had conducted for the Social Security Administration, Medicare, Small Business Administration, and Coast Guard. These assessments considered four dimensions: the identification of manpower requirements (more specifically, the skills and knowledge needed by the organization to meets its objectives), the size of the manpower inventory (more specifically, the skills and knowledge on hand, so that the gap between requirements and inventory can be determined), the workforce strategies and plans needed to close the gap, and the ongoing assessment and improvement of the strategies and plans when implemented (McClure, 2001).

As part of the discussion, GAO noted that the Coast Guard has been deficient in knowing its human capital requirements and partially deficient in knowing its human capital inventory. The GAO reported, for example, that the Coast Guard's Office of Force Management, responsible for "identifying, evaluating, and analyzing all IT personnel requirements and ensuring that performance qualifications meet mission needs," nonetheless had "not assessed the knowledge and skills needed by its civilian IT workforce." Moreover, the Coast Guard did "not have a complete inventory of IT knowledge and skills." Although the

---

[6] See Davis, 2001. . The 425,000 figure probably came from an ITAA (2001) report released in the spring.

[7] Later in the hearings, Mark Forman, representing the Office of Management and Budget, stated that the Bush Administration would soon submit legislation to seek "enhanced authority to use recruitment and retention bonuses, permit agencies to easily develop demonstration projects and implement alternative personnel systems, authorize managers to use workforce restructuring tools including early retirement packages and buyouts, and recruit and treat senior executives more comparably with their private sector counterparts." See the testimony of Mark Forman (2001).

Coast Guard had policies and procedures for addressing gaps between requirements and inventory, since it "had not yet fully defined the IT skills and knowledge needed by its civilian workforce," it did not have a strategy for meeting those needs. Neither had the Coast Guard's Office of Management "analyzed or reported on the effectiveness of its specific recruiting, training, and incentive programs" (McClure, 2001).

Testimony at the same hearing from the Office of Personnel Management (OPM) (Winstead, 2001) focused on what OPM recognized as certain inadequacies in the federal compensation system that would affect the recruitment and retention of qualified IT personnel. These inadequacies, which were documented in a report prepared by the National Academy of Public Administration (NAPA), included[8]

- "too much emphasis on internal equity and too little sensitivity to the market"
- too little recognition of individual performance (referred to in the NAPA report as "contribution equity")
- too little flexibility to adjust to market wage dynamics at a government-wide level.

On behalf of OPM, Winstead (2001) testified that steps were being taken to respond to these inadequacies, however. Specifically, 7 to 33 percent salary rate increases for federal IT workers took effect in January 2001, and OPM issued a new IT classification standard.

Other testimonies also described steps taken to improve the recruitment of IT personnel. Donald Upson, Secretary of Technology of the Commonwealth of Virginia, testified (2001) that Virginia had recently revamped and modernized its personnel management and compensation system, reducing its legacy system of 1,650 job classifications to 300, including 11 in IT career fields. Salaries in the IT fields were increased, and broad pay bands ensured that workers would not have to become supervisors to receive a large pay increase. Virginia offered its workers expanded opportunity for telecommuting; tuition assistance; greater training opportunities; hiring and retention bonuses of up to $10,000; up to 30 days vacation for new or incumbent employees; an open-ended window within which to use compensatory time; salary adjustments of up to 10 percent for retention, internal alignment, or for learning and applying new skills; and higher percentage increases for promotions.

Not everyone at the hearing was convinced of the existence of a recruiting problem in IT fields. In a dissenting view, Colleen Kelley (2001), president of the National Treasury Employees Union, stated (among other things) that the problem in federal government IT personnel organization was not the lack of flexibility in the federal compensation and management system, but the lack of funding to allow managers to implement the flexibility. According to Kelley's testimony, agencies can "offer retention allowances of up to 25% of salary, bonuses of up to 25% of basic pay, performance awards, student loan repayment awards, incentive awards and even bilingual awards." She added that in December of 1999, the Office of Personnel Management reported that overall,

> only 1.4% of all Executive Branch employees received recruitment, retention or relocation incentives (3Rs) in FY 1998. Recruitment bonuses were given 0.3% of the time. Relocation bonuses were given to 1.0 percent of employees and 0.09% of em-

---

[8] See NAPA, 2001. Winstead's testimony (2001) points out that the NAPA report was "part of a cooperative effort by NAPA, the Chief Information Officers Council, the Human Resources Management Council, and the Office of Personnel Management to improve the government's ability to attract and keep top quality information technology workers."

ployees received retention allowances. Less than 1/4 of 1% of the federal workforce received any form of recruitment, retention or relocation incentive in FY 1998 (Kelley, 2001).

IT Careers in the Military

Judging by the military IT occupations cited in U.S. Office of the Secretary of Defense, 1999, and our review of the literature on this topic, there are substantial opportunities in IT occupations for both enlisted members and officers. Enlisted IT members establish, operate, and maintain networks, serve as systems administrators, operate and maintain small computers, and process data. Officers in IT occupations concern themselves with higher-level activities of systems design, telecommunications, command and control, information warfare, and the provision of information. We can expect that IT occupations are, like other military occupations, designed around a set of core tasks that have been defined by the training community working in conjunction with the end users. The training community also defines the skills and knowledge required to perform the core tasks and determines which of the tasks should be taught in advanced individual training and which should be learned on the job.

The opportunity to learn and use basic computer skills is presumably a strong attraction for IT enlisted recruits, particularly considering the private-sector value of these skills. Military members can also have their IT skills certified and can obtain additional IT training through private providers. These opportunities increase the transferability of IT skills acquired through military service and increase the attractiveness for recruits of entering into such fields. For instance, Military-To-Work is a web site that targets ex-military personnel for IT and communications jobs. The site, piloted in the spring of 1999, was developed by the Communications Workers of America with a grant from the Department of Labor and backed by several corporations (US West Communications, AT&T, and Bell Atlantic). Also, Microsoft offers certification for systems administration and for systems engineer. The Microsoft web site provides information and links. The Microsoft Military IT Career program was available nationwide in 1999 at 160 bases and posts, with training costs ranging from $200 for books for the self-paced option to $1,000–$2,000 for each instructor-led course. There are online aptitude tests, and "service members may use Montgomery GI Bill and Tuition Assistance to finance training expenses" (see Vincent, 1999).

A high rate of change in IT means a high rate of obsolescence of IT human capital. Given a high rate of obsolescence, a worker's stock of IT human capital will grow only if the rate of investment is high and geared to the latest hardware and software. To the extent that military IT is up-to-date, the IT education and training provided by the military can be transferred to the private sector. But while the transferability of training thus can have a positive influence on recruitment, it may have a negative influence on retention if recruits leave the military early in their careers to pursue civilian jobs.[9]

The growth of IT has given impetus to the restructuring of military occupations. These changes have typically focused on simplifying and consolidating IT occupations. For

[9] This observation was echoed in our interviews, and we consider it when modeling the supply of IT personnel in Chapter Six.

instance, the Army restructured its Signal Corps military occupational specialties (MOSs) in 1997 and 1998, reducing the number of enlisted specialties from 50 to 18 and additional skill identifiers from 60 to 11. Maj. Gen. Michael Ackerman, commanding general of the Signal Center and School, Fort Gordon, expected the number of MOSs to fall even further "because of technological advancements that will allow certain equipment-specific specialties to be merged" ("Recent Restructuring Puts Signal Corps in Good Health," 1998). As another example, in the late 1990s the Navy merged two enlisted ratings—data processing (DP) and radioman (RM), ultimately creating a new rating, information systems technician—which became the largest single source of enlisted IT personnel in the Navy. The Navy also created several new Naval Enlisted Classification (NEC) codes associated with specific skill requirements within the IT rating. These include information systems administrator (NEC 2735), network security vulnerability technician (NEC 2780), information systems security manager (NEC 2779), and advanced network analyst (NEC 2781). The information systems administrator was targeted toward pay grades E-4 and E-5, while the others were targeted on E-5 to E-8, E-7 to E-9, and E-6 to E-8, respectively.[10]

The consolidation of military IT occupations has raised the question of whether U.S. military forces could benefit from using a cadre of highly trained IT professionals capable of fostering rapid innovations as needed. The Israeli armed forces have made such a move through the creation of the Israeli Army's computer corps, or Mamram:

> In a country where all 18-year-olds are drafted for a minimum two years of military service, the computer corps skims only the cream, rejecting 9 out of 10 applicants. Once in, recruits train for six months and must commit themselves to a six-year tour of duty. And while computer specialists are not run ragged on 50-mile forced marches, they endure 16-hour days and a failure rate that runs as high as 50 percent. Instead of the M-16 assault rifles carried by combat soldiers, rookies at the military's programming school in Ramat Gan, suburb of Tel Aviv, are taught to cherish their laptop and hand-held computers. "You won't find anyone here who says the course is easy," said Maj. Shai Bassan, the computer corps–training commander, as a classroom of 40 students clicked away at a programming exercise. "They are in a race in the framework of a commando unit," the major said. "They know only the best will remain," and join the elite corps. Those who survive the training at Ramat Gan spend time developing programs for everything from how to feed 10,000 soldiers efficiently to software that encodes communications for air strikes against Islamic militant guerilla bases in Lebanon. Company recruiters are also aggressively trying to hire army programmers because they manage projects using advanced technology that their age-group peers cannot get near in civilian industry ("Israeli Army Computer Corps Builds Success in Business," 1999).

Whether it would make sense for the U.S. to amalgamate its IT occupations into an IT corps is an open question. The U.S. military is considerably larger and may find it more efficient to offer more IT tracks, each with a different kind of skill specialization.[11] Also, the

---

[10] U.S. Office of the Secretary of Defense, 1999, pp. F-13–F-16. The report also provides other examples of how the services restructured or created new IT occupations.

[11] The Navy officer corps has created a new primary designator ("community") called the Information Profession (IP) community, with its own career path and structure. This community will be responsible for administering and managing information technology in the Navy. It appears that the Navy may be moving closer to the Israeli Army approach of a separate IT corps. We thank Stephen Mehay for this point.

military may find it effective to rely more on outside contractors or commercial off-the-shelf applications for programming than to follow Israel's example.

Observations

This survey of the relevant literature, popular press, and congressional studies on the topic of IT and the IT workforce suggests that personnel development and management is central to the quality and effectiveness of IT workers and is especially significant for the military services in their competition with private-sector firms.

Economic analyses are at last detecting the strong influence of IT on economic growth. The increase in computing power and the decrease in computing cost have been nothing short of phenomenal, and this has spurred the dissemination of IT throughout the economy. Economists have referred to IT as a general purpose technology that facilitates *innovation* in a host of areas, which leads to new products and more efficient processes, and which subsequently feeds back to increase the demand for further advances in IT. Given the many military activities that are counterparts to those in the civilian economy, the potential for advances in military applications seems equally large.

Economists also argue that the widespread diffusion of IT throughout the economy has contributed to the increased wage dispersion in the private sector. IT appears to be a complement for skills requiring knowledge and judgment and a substitute for repetitive activities and rote-knowledge skills. Wages rose more rapidly in the 1980s and early 1990s for workers with more education. Wages also became more disperse within a level of education, apparently as deeper knowledge and better judgment revealed on the job were rewarded.

Looking more closely at the attitudes of the IT workforce itself, our literature analysis suggested that IT workers in the private sector want access to the latest hardware and software, regular training to keep their skills up to date, flexible schedules that allow them to balance professional life and private life, challenges that keep them motivated (such as a chance to work on hot projects), and the commitment of their employer to help them build an exciting career. During the late-90s boom, IT workers were in high demand in the private sector. Their reportedly high pay, however, often came with long hours and little flexibility in their schedules. Moreover, the widely held view of a large shortage in the supply of IT workers, stretching well into this decade, was evidently mistaken.

Indeed, our literature review raised questions surrounding this reported shortage of IT workers, whether in the private or public sectors. Although the literature in several instances described concerns about such a shortage, in other instances it provided evidence that any such shortage might not be as likely or as severe as estimated. In fact, as noted previously, Lerman's analysis showed that the inflow of college graduates would likely meet the then-anticipated growth in demand for IT workers. On net, the demand for IT workers can probably be described as a component of the demand for well-educated, high-aptitude workers.

The literature suggested that the compensation, management, and development of IT workers in the federal government were important to the successful recruitment and retention of high-quality IT employees. Several studies suggested that IT personnel management, especially in the public sector, had been hamstrung by an inadequate classification of IT jobs, an excess of jobs classifications, too little flexibility in pay levels and pay growth, and limited access to new hardware, software, and training. However, the literature also suggested that the federal government had recognized these issues and taken steps toward improvement.

For the military, IT training was found to play a crucial role in enhancing the attractiveness of IT positions to potential recruits. However, because of the value of IT skills in the civilian sector, IT training also presents a challenge to personnel retention. We will return to this possible contradiction in a later chapter.

Like other complex technology, IT hardware, software, and communications can be adapted to, and evolved for, particular applications in a way that simplifies their installation, use, maintenance, and repair. Therefore, the application of this inherently complex technology typically does not require highly specialized engineers and technicians, although they typically are required to invent, innovate, adapt, and evolve the technology for the application. By implication, the military's growing reliance on IT does not necessarily imply an increase in the percentage of force members who are IT specialists, or in their education, training, and aptitude requirements. This is not to say that adapting IT to particular uses is done correctly the first time, that all uses are foreseen at the time of first adaptation, or that high demand for IT specialists will be a one-time event. However, the cycle of research, development, test, evaluation, and subsequent field use and feedback, with further adaptation, seems as well suited to IT as to other technologies used by the military. If so, we see the importance of having creative, capable leadership and personnel engaged in the transformation of the force—who envision the need for future capabilities; define prototypes, specifications, and probable doctrine; and oversee the range of activities from invention to test to acquisition.

CHAPTER THREE

Evidence from Field Interviews on the Management of Enlisted IT Occupations

Although the observations drawn from recent literature and the popular press provide insight into the characteristics of both private- and public-sector IT occupations, a more practical and applied understanding of the IT sector and its personnel organization is also needed. To explore the existing IT personnel management structure in the armed forces and its potential for future flexibility and adaptation, we conducted field interviews with officers and enlisted members. We had hoped to gain a firsthand perspective on the connection between long-term visions of a transformed force heavily reliant on IT, on the one hand, and short-term IT manpower requirements on the other. We were particularly interested in IT manpower requirements in future force structures, how the requirements were determined, and how manpower planning connected the long-term requirements with short-term IT manpower needs.

The interviews were not extensive and provided only limited information about these questions. Although we heard reports of a shortage of IT personnel and gained information about manpower problems in specific occupations, we were not able to obtain a precise assessment of future force IT manpower needs. However, one of the most important implications of the information we did uncover on these issues is the recognition that, in many respects, it is not feasible for the services to predict the precise numbers of IT workers or types of IT activities that it will demand in the distant future. Both the nature of the military and the dominant characteristics of IT as a field (e.g., its broad scope, rapid change, and the many occupations that may be considered IT related) make it difficult to forecast future force structure or needs.[1] The military cannot predict what kinds of new technology will materialize years from now, how applications based on the new technology will be incorporated into the armed forces, or what kinds of manpower will be needed by the applications.

However, the military's inability to make such predictions successfully does not mean that its recruitment and retention policies will be unable to attract sufficient personnel or maintain an adequately qualified force. To the contrary, we recognized during the course of the interviews and research that it is more useful to study the flexibility and adaptability of the IT management structure and the personnel development policies. Fluidity and responsiveness in these areas can allow the armed forces to meet their manpower needs, regardless of what they might be. The information provided in our interviews, though not precisely what we were originally searching for, is pertinent because it sheds light on the extent of such

[1] Other analysts have reached the same conclusion. "During the next 30 years, the Navy will introduce several new platforms. New technologies on the future platform will automate many routine tasks and information processing functions that sailors currently perform. . . . How will sailors' jobs change? Of course, we will not know the full extent of automation on manpower requirements until ships' designs are complete" (Golding, Arkes, and Koopman, 1999, p. 5).

flexibility within the services, the characteristics of current IT management, and the potential for future adaptation of many different types.

In this chapter, we first explain our methodology in conducting the interviews. Then we present findings on the management of IT and IT-related personnel in the Army, examining the process for generating manpower requirements for these career fields, assessing the overall health of units, and identifying incentives for enlistment and reenlistment as well as incentives for soldiers to obtain additional education and training. We then present findings on similar issues for the Air Force specialties and offer observations and conclusions.

Methodology

Because of project budget and time considerations, our interviews focused on the U.S. Army and the U.S. Air Force. We selected relevant MOSs in the Army. The MOSs chosen were represented by information systems (career management field [CMF] 74, also known as signals) and military intelligence (CMF 96). We also selected comparable Air Force specialty codes (AFSCs), namely, the 3C series (communications-computer systems operations) and AFSC 1N series (operations intelligence).

We view intelligence as IT related for two main reasons. First, signal intelligence seems to fit naturally within the IT classification, given its heavy use of IT systems. The other aspect of intelligence, human intelligence, can also be interpreted as an IT occupation, because it includes not only the gathering of information through interrogation, but also the compilation and access to that information, which are assisted now by IT.

We identified offices within the services and specific individuals responsible for determining the manpower requirements of these specialties and for the management of personnel in these specialties. Typically, these individuals were in the personnel and training commands, as opposed to the operating commands; however, the process used to determine manpower requirements is similar in the different commands. Below we provide more detailed information about the structure of the Army and Air Force specialties and the individuals and offices we contacted.

Army

Signals (CMF 74) houses the computer systems security and other computer-related jobs. Most of the basic and advanced formal training for signals is done at Ft. Gordon, Georgia. For intelligence (CMF 96), basic and advanced formal training occurs at Ft. Huachuca, Arizona. CMFs 74 and 96 include the following specialties:

- 74B information systems operator/analyst
- 74C telecommunications operator/maintainer
- 74G (which has been closed and merged with 74B)
- 74Z information systems chief (the capstone MOS for CMF 74)
- 96B intelligence analyst
- 96D imagery analyst
- 96H ground surveillance radar operator
- 96R imagery ground station operation

- 96U unmanned aerial vehicle operator
- 96Z military intelligence chief (the capstone occupation for CMF 96).

The Army's general procedure for ascertaining the training and manpower requirements for a CMF is known as the CMF review. This review occurs quarterly through an inter-command process that brings together high-level military and civilian managerial personnel from the personnel, education, and training commands. The CMF review evaluates recruiting and retention goals and determines course and skill requirements for the CMF. The CMF review is also responsible for monitoring the overall health of the CMF.

We met with personnel from each command that fed into the CMF review process and with personnel responsible for managing individuals in specific MOSs. These were, for the most part, senior noncommissioned officers (NCOs) and, in some instances, civilians. For example, we spoke with several civilians involved in developing the training requirements for soldiers in the Signal Corps.

Air Force

We studied Air Force specialties that most closely resembled the skill sets in Army signals and intelligence, namely, the AFSC 3C series (communications-computer systems operations) and the AFSC 1N series (operations intelligence). Unlike the Army, which monitors the full spectrum of requirements and manning of its CMFs quarterly, the Air Force handles its personnel issues with a process called the Utilization and Training Workshop (U&TW). The U&TW conducts, among other things, an in-depth analysis of occupational requirements and instructional system requirements for the career field (Robbert et al., unpublished). While the U&TW appears to address many of the same issues as the CMF review, the U&TW occurs over a cycle of *several years* rather than several months. We endeavored to understand the components of the U&TW and to meet with offices and individuals involved in this process.

Structured Interviews

For all the interviews, we used a semistructured format that considered several topics:

- formal educational opportunities available to personnel
- informal or on-the-job training opportunities available to personnel
- available noncompensation incentives to encourage personnel to obtain more skills
- extant compensation and management tools that enable the services to recruit, retain, and promote its pool of knowledge workers.

Because the Army and Air Force processes are not identical, the interviews illuminated different kinds of information and data for these two services.

Army Interviews

Our discussion with Army CMF managers revealed challenges relating to the retention of skilled, qualified IT personnel, but also suggested that the Army does have a rather thorough IT planning and training process, which is able to successfully develop the required IT workforce. In addition, our interviewees were able to shed light on the effectiveness, prevalence, and limitations of the existing training and incentive programs. Such information implies that although an array of recruitment, retention, and personnel development strategies are used throughout the Army IT occupations, there is room for improvement in the application of these incentives, improvement that would assist the Army in reaching its future force IT needs and expectations.

IT Manpower in the Future Force: Requirements Generation Process

Our interviewees offered observations about the specific steps within the requirement generation process as well as the actions taken to make sure that a given unit is able to meet its future force requirements and train its personnel. This information is useful to understand the sufficiency of future IT manpower because it provides a description of the factors and procedures that go into planning for the IT needs of the transforming Army.

The requirement generation process occurs separately for each major command in each service. In the Army, a biennial process called Total Army Analysis is the basis for the determination of future manpower needs. There are four phases within the procedure. The first, force guidance, uses guidance from several sources, including the National Military Strategy, the Defense Planning Guidance, the Army Plan, as well as resource assumptions and priorities, to develop a theater force structure. Next, in the quantitative analysis phase, the proposed force is run through several computer simulations. Qualitative analysis, the third phase, identifies potential constraints, develops a plan to achieve the desired force structure, and specifies the numbers and types of units. Finally, in the leadership review phase, the proposed force is reviewed and approved by the Secretary of the Army and the Vice Chief of Staff (Reece, Holt, and Trotter, 1993).

There is a difference between the requirement generation processes for combat units and those for support units. Combat units are described in terms of a table of organization and equipment, and after input from the field from individual unit commanders, a modified table of organization and equipment is determined. In contrast, support activities are described in a table of distributions and allowances. After this point, however, both types of positions use the same process to determine specific manpower requirements. Using OPTEMPO (the operational tempo required) for mission capability, an appropriate workload is determined, engineered standards are used to calculate the number of man-hours inherent in that workload, and these man-hours are converted to number of people.[2] It is then up to the CMF managers and their individual review processes to meet the proposed manpower levels.

Most generally, the CMF review process is used to develop a program or agenda for managing the accession, development, and training of personnel. In this process, the Personnel Command (PERSCOM) is responsible for monitoring and evaluating trends in enlistment, attrition, and retention and for determining whether their targets are being met. It is also PERSCOM's job to understand why soldiers enter, remain in, or leave service. Problems that are identified are vetted through the CMF process in conjunction with the Training and Doctrine Command (TRADOC). More broadly, the CMF review is intended to take account of the expected mission of the specific career field as well as the manpower authoriza-

---

[2] "Force Accounting and System Division," 2003, offers a clear explanation of the requirement determination process, which, while in this case specific to the Training and Doctrine Command, is essentially the same for other commands.

tions required in the near future (e.g., those due to changes in equipment or system upgrades), and to anticipate downstream manning requirements. The CMF review should also ensure that requirements and resources are synchronized such that training resources are available when needed.

Interviewees at Ft. Huachuca explained that the CMF managers were essential to personnel management and to the attainment of manpower and training needs. They oversee specialties in their CMFs, work with trainers to ensure that necessary skills are imparted, and work with recruiters to ensure that they are attracting the personnel needed to meet manpower and aptitude requirements. CMF managers also work with PERSCOM to ensure that personnel policies mesh with the needs of the CMF. The managers, who understand the needs of the CMF, must interact with policymakers and assignment personnel to make sure everyone recognizes the key issues in the CMF. They are also responsible for monitoring data on recruiting, retention, and training and for contacting the Department of the Army to obtain reenlistment or enlistment bonuses when these incentives are necessary to maintain the health of the CMF.

Another process, the Structure Manning Decision Review, is used to determine instructional needs for personnel. The Structure Manning Decision Review is convened annually and attended by the Department of the Army, TRADOC, and the functional proponents that make use of the trained personnel. The review uses a four-year time horizon and must ensure that training resources are built in the program objective memorandum, which serves to connect resource programming with plans and objectives. The Structure Manning Decision Review plans for major hardware changes and for the skill sets required by these changes. Efforts are made to focus the skill requirements of the MOS on its mission rather than tying the MOS and its skill set to particular pieces of equipment, which will certainly change over time.

With respect to the military intelligence (MI) CMF, the review occurs quarterly and involves representatives from Ft. Huachuca (the MI "school house"), PERSCOM, and organizations in Crystal City, such as the Defense Intelligence Agency. Our interviewees indicated that the determination of MI manpower requirements seemed to be driven by TRADOC, which designs the courses to be taken by MI personnel, and overseen by the Office of Chief, Military Intelligence (OCMI). According to interlocutors at Ft. Huachuca, it is the job of OCMI to "keep an eye on the life cycle of the MOS." Changes in requirements, as determined by TRADOC and OCMI, are communicated to PERSCOM, whose job is to identify soldiers with the appropriate skills and aptitude, i.e., the faces to fill the spaces. There are also opportunities to receive feedback from the "consumers" of the soldiers produced by this process (e.g., the Fourth Infantry Division at Ft. Hood).

Interviewees at Ft. Gordon explained that in order to devise a program to meet manpower requirements in the signals CMF, a board is convened from various units involved in signals training and from the consumer community that requires the trained personnel. This board convenes apart from the CMF review process. The board typically meets at least every two years but more frequently in the event of rapid change or unexpected developments. For example, when a new system or a new hardware item appears, the board develops and promulgates a series of approved tasks for it. Often, a private-sector firm (or materials developer) develops the tasks under contract. The board subsequently reviews and approves the tasks or requests changes as needed. The board also decides the venue of the training, i.e., whether it will be provided at the unit level or in a training facility.

This type of review process gives the consumer community the necessary information to provide feedback to the board. Concerns, perceived needs, or other issues affecting the consumer community are aired at a board meeting or communicated to board members by other means, enabling the board to evaluate requirements determination with some understanding of the users' perspectives.

Assessing the Overall Health of the Unit: Recruitment and Retention

After gaining some understanding of requirement determination, our next task was to consider the overall health of the unit. In making this assessment, we focused on the sufficiency of the unit's manpower and its ability to meet recruitment and retention goals.

We found that the majority of CMF units were adequately staffed and had at least come close to their accession/retention goals. For example, the NCOs with whom we discussed the overall standing of CMF 74 generally described it as healthy. MOSs 74B and 74C had reportedly met their accession goals for fiscal year (FY) 2001. Although retention in 74B was initially low compared with that in the Army overall, it rose during the fiscal year, and 74C had experienced no accession or retention problems. We note that retention in the unit was being compared with overall Army averages, not targets specific to the CMF or its MOSs.[3]

Despite CMF 74 being generally healthy, the interviewees mentioned specific problems that affected the management of personnel. For example, there was a reported shortfall of soldiers with a top-secret clearance resulting in insufficient manpower to fill special assignments. The problem was exacerbated by lengthy delays of 12 months or longer in obtaining a top-secret clearance.[4] In 74C, the biggest shortfall occurred in obtaining qualified personnel to fill billets in the Special Operations Command, where such a clearance is needed. We should note that, although there is no specific connection between the clearance issue and the IT occupations, IT skills are often used in secret or top-secret work. As a result, the lack of IT personnel with the appropriate clearance poses a substantial, though unexpected, obstacle to meeting IT manpower requirements.

An analysis of another MOS, 74Z, known as a low-density MOS because it contains a relatively small number of personnel, reveals that retention is a significant concern for this unit. As a capstone MOS, accession targets are not relevant (a capstone MOS is fed from subordinate MOSs), but at the time of our interviews, retention was slightly below the Army-wide average. We were told that retaining 74Zs was difficult because their technical skills were in demand by private industry. Retirement eligibility was also cited as a factor worsening retention in this MOS.[5]

Our interviews with CMF 96 yielded similar observations and highlighted retention as the key challenge for maintaining an adequate number and quality of personnel. While CMF 96 was at the Army average in meeting its enlistment target, retention was a notable problem, particularly for soldiers at mid-career (E-5 and E-6). Our interviewees in this CMF felt that the low retention rate could partly be explained by the fact that many MI soldiers entered for the educational benefits (e.g., the Montgomery G.I. Bill and the College Fund)

---

[3] See CMF 74 Review, current as of April 3, 2001, available from U.S. Army PERSCOM.

[4] Ibid.

[5] Ibid.

and left at the end of their term to begin using the benefits.[6] Furthermore, our interviewees suggested that low retention rates in this specialty might also result from "poaching" by the civilian contractors who conducted the All Source Analyst System course and provided information on outside earnings, which enticed some servicemen to seek alternate employment in the private sector.

Research at Ft. Huachuca offered further perspective on the retention challenge. In our interviews, we were told that MI personnel had a distinct lack of incentive to make a career of the Army. This had a trickle-down effect: The loss of experienced soldiers caused a speed-up in promoting junior personnel to fill the emptied billets. As a result, those who were promoted lacked experience and skills necessary to train more-junior personnel. Overall, the mission suffered as overall experience dropped. Our interlocutors noted that they were even losing people at the 15-year mark, just five years before eligibility for military retirement. This implies that, for some personnel at least, the disincentives to remaining in an IT occupation in the Army—or the lure of civilian job opportunities—were great enough to dominate military retirement benefits and retired military health benefits, eligibility for both of which occurs at 20 years of service.

As in CMF 74, the long lag in obtaining a top-secret clearance was an impediment to managing soldiers in CMF 96. Even before September 11, 2001, the backlog was 14 months if the file contained no derogatory information and longer otherwise. Ft. Huachuca cannot keep a soldier until the clearance comes, however; so after some period the soldier receives an interim clearance and is assigned to a unit. If the clearance is denied, the soldier is processed for termination or reclassified into another MOS. During the background review for the clearance, the soldier remains in the MOS and counts against its authorized manning. Such personnel compose 3–5 percent of the overall trained inventory.

Although reclassification can move a soldier from MI into another specialty, reclassification into MI is difficult and is not an effective way to smooth manning shortfalls. For example, a sergeant first class seeking to reclassify would lack the knowledge base to be effective in MI. In contrast, a junior soldier reclassifying into MI begins with advanced individual training and builds the knowledge base. A reclassifying staff sergeant goes to the basic noncommissioned officer course, which provides some of the training needed for MI, but if the sergeant has already taken the basic noncommissioned officers course (BNCOC), retaking it is not required, even though about 50 percent of the BNCOC content is specific to the occupation.

Speaking specifically about recruitment and retention, interlocutors at Ft. Huachuca said that changes in MI-related specialties should have led the Army to become more innovative in the way it recruits for these specialties, but it had not. Furthermore, many interlocutors expressed dissatisfaction that retention targets were gauged to the overall Army average, since they felt that the overall average was not relevant to the mission of a particular spe-

---

[6] According to the Veterans Administration, which administers the Montgomery G.I. Bill (MGIB), soldiers may use the benefit until ten years from the date of last discharge or release from active duty. This is a new feature of the MGIB program. Previously, individuals could use the benefit up to ten years after becoming eligible for the MGIB. Thus, under the old rules, soldiers *had* to leave service before the benefit expired in order to use it. Often this would happen after the first term. Under the new guidance, soldiers do not have to separate after the first term to maximize use of the benefit. See "The Montgomery GI Bill-Active Duty," at www.gibill.va.gov/education/c30pam.htm#_Toc518285755, last accessed September 2, 2003.

cialty. It would be more helpful, they suggested, to track the fill rate of an MOS against its authorized manning.

Recruitment and Retention: Incentives for Enlistment and Reenlistment

To meet MI requirements and those for IT personnel in other MOSs, the Army uses enlistment and reenlistment bonuses to attract and retain high-quality or highly skilled personnel. Bonuses allow the services to respond quickly to shortfalls in retention.[7] However, despite the effectiveness of such bonuses in other areas of the Army, their use in the units that we interviewed was surprisingly limited. Furthermore, there was a lack of readily accessible information on the nature of enlistment and reenlistment bonuses, their size, and the requirements for receiving them.

There are many examples of the limited incentives used in these units. For example, MOSs 74B and 74C did not have an enlistment bonus or Army College Fund at the time of the interviews. MOS 74B had a selective reenlistment bonus (SRB), and 74C had a targeted SRB (TSRB) for assignments to Korea and Ft. Bragg. Despite the challenge of retaining 74Zs, it did not have an SRB or TSRB. CMF 96 had no enlistment bonus and no second-term reenlistment bonus (no "zone B" bonus). It is true, however, that CMF 96 had become a "STAR" MOS, meaning that promotions could be made as needed to fill vacant positions. When combined with the strong economy and the presence of personnel recruiters eager to hire bright, well-trained soldiers like those in MI, the lack of reenlistment bonuses contributed to the manning shortfall, particularly at the E-5/E-6 level. In fact, their manning was at 83 percent of authorized billets, as compared with full or nearly full manning for more-junior and more-senior billets in the CMF.

Many interviewees suggested that the opportunity to reclassify into a specialty with faster promotion or better civilian job opportunities could be used as an accession or reenlistment incentive. Currently, some soldiers can reclassify into CMF 74 or move between specialties within CMF 74. Soldiers who reclassify receive the training required for their CMF 74 specialty. Within CMF 74, soldiers may be more attracted to 74B than 74C because 74B is perceived to be more marketable. In addition, interviewees in PERSCOM said 74B had a relatively fast speed of promotion because its first-term reenlistment rate was low. A motivated soldier could reach E-6 by the end of a four- to six-year initial commitment in 74B, indicating a very fast rate of promotion. But in the main, the Army did not encourage reclassifying, except for low-density, hard-to-fill specialties, and reclassification remains a limited instrument for motivating reenlistment. Our research suggests that expanded reclassification opportunities could be interpreted as an indirect form of compensation and motivation to attract qualified soldiers into the CMF and into 74B in particular.

Personnel Management and Retention: Incentives for Education and Training

Education and training are two final aspects of the IT personnel management structure that we investigated during our interviews. Although there are few direct, monetary incentives for obtaining additional training, personnel who gain additional skills increase their opportuni-

---

[7] The services can allocate bonus funds across specialties as they see fit. Thus, bonuses are a flexible and rapidly applied compensation tool. When retention conditions grow unexpectedly worse, however, the bonus budget may be too small to shore up retention. The services may then have to wait for the passage of the next authorization and appropriation bills for more money. Still, the pace of response can be slower on the DoD civilian side. The dot-com boom had nearly ended by the time DoD received special pay rates for IT civilians.

ties for promotion and the range of possible future assignments. Our interviews suggested that educational incentives could be more effectively employed as a retention tool, particularly in the IT sector. In fact, a number of interviewees noted that although educational opportunities existed for soldiers, they were not used as explicit incentives for a soldier to stay in the military. For example, soldiers can draw MGIB and college funds even before they qualify (by completing three consecutive years of service), and they might be willing to accept longer service obligations in exchange for higher educational benefits. Our interlocutors argued that educational opportunities should be employed more explicitly as an incentive to stay in the military beyond the first term.

Many of the Army's channels of education and training are controlled by PERSCOM: advanced individual training (AIT), the professional leadership development course, the BNCOC, the advanced noncommissioned officers course (ANCOC), and the sergeant major academy.

The unit pays for some types of training, including training in the global command and control system for joint and coalition forces, and other institutional and special skills training in the case of CMF 74. For these specifically identified skills, soldiers are selected for training based on their drive, capability, and the training needs of the unit.

Soldier management and training in a CMF is the responsibility of a professional development NCO and an assignment manager. The professional development NCO helps direct soldiers to training required for advancement. For instance, MOS 96B requires the Battle Staff Course for those who are E-6 and above. Personnel may be sent to training by the unit or sent en route to the unit by PERSCOM. One of the newest requirements was the All Source Analyst System training, which was needed by about 10 percent of 96B.

A large portion of IT training was outsourced and used commercial off-the-shelf educational materials, making the skills acquired applicable to a range of military assignments as well as private-sector opportunities. According to interviewees at Ft. Gordon, the training school for signals, frequently commercial vendors taught the fundamentals of operating systems, whether they were Microsoft, Sun Solaris, Unix, or other systems. Military trainers were using commercial curricula as well. Such training is beneficial because it allows soldiers to receive certification for the skills they learned, thus increasing the transferability of IT skills and making the IT position more attractive. Skill certification was being actively encouraged, with funding available from the unit and with programs allowing the soldier to certify but providing incentives for retention. One such program, certification for Cisco routers, took about eight weeks for a civilian to complete. The Army created a program giving the first two weeks of this training in AIT, the next three weeks in BNCOC, and the remainder in ANCOC. Staged training like this might be an effective tool to recruit and retain soldiers, but since the time span in a military career from AIT to ANCOC is about eight years, the incentive to take this training in the Army seems weak. This program aside, most of the training (75–95 percent) at Ft. Gordon was industry based. Although soldiers placed a high value on certification, they often did not receive it.

Interviewees also noted some negative aspects of commercial-based, outsourced training, particularly with regard to personnel retention. Interviewees were concerned about the use of private contractors to provide training for systems such as Tactical Unmanned Aerial Vehicle and PROPHET (a modified military automotive vehicle with equipment to detect signals and the direction of their origin) since they felt that these trainers exploited their interaction with military personnel to identify promising employment candidates and to provide them with information about outside pay and opportunities.[8]

Additional training can also complicate the issue of retention, given that training often qualifies personnel for lucrative private-sector opportunities and that the Army cannot reward individuals quid pro quo (e.g., promotion in exchange for undergoing training.) Furthermore, there can be a significant and costly lag between when training occurs and when it can be applied. For example, a trained soldier often cannot be assigned to a new system because it is not yet available. We were told that a temporary increase in promotions could have counteracted these concerns, but more promotions would have required an increase in authorized billets at higher grades. The interviewees noted the value of having a current surplus of mid-level and senior NCOs to ensure sufficient future supply of senior NCOs. They suggested a 25 percent surplus as a buffer for manning legacy systems as well as new systems, because these come on line sporadically.

Our interviews suggested that an increase in pay for IT and MI specialists who undergo additional training might make them more satisfied with their assignments and encourage them to stay in the military. However, interviewees reported that only indirect incentives existed to induce specialists to pursue such additional training, except in the case of language proficiency pay for certain MI specialties. For example, individuals who take additional courses may be perceived as having a high level of motivation, which is considered in promotion decisions. In some cases, courses or training are required for promotion and hence higher pay. Also, additional skills may expand the range of assignments for which a member is considered, which should increase the chance that the member will be satisfied with the assignment. Finally, interviewees at Ft. Gordon indicated that while special pay had been proposed for IT personnel in signal specialties, the Army made no provision for this in its proposed budget. Interviewees cited federal occupational code 334, which allows federal civilian employees to receive special pay, as an example for the military to follow. Such a policy, adapted to fit the needs of the military, might improve reenlistment.

Key Issues

Overall, our interviews with Army personnel suggested that training and educational incentives, though underused, are essential tools in the management, recruitment, and retention of IT personnel. The interviews indicated that valuable IT training appears to be a significant factor in the choice to enlist and could be better orchestrated to maximize retention. However, our discussions also implied that retention remains a significant challenge because of the imperative of meeting manpower requirements and, for trained personnel, because of the attractiveness of outside opportunities.

Our interviews also demonstrated that the Army does indeed have a system in place to assess current and near-term manpower needs and to plan for appropriate IT personnel training and development. The increasing use of commercial IT products, training, and certification was cited as evidence of the Army's attempt to more effectively develop and retain

[8] Interviewees expressed other objections to the use of contractors, although some of these topics are beyond the scope of this research. Some interviewees argued that civilian instructors do not compare favorably with military instructors who go into the field and return with firsthand knowledge to instruct students. Moreover, detractors of outsourcing argued that private-sector instructors could teach only doctrine, not employment. This argument has merit, but many instructors are former members of the military.

its IT personnel. Enlistment and reenlistment bonuses and reclassification were additional incentives suggested as mechanisms to attract and keep qualified personnel.

We draw three primary conclusions from our interviews. First, the requirements generation process appears to be generally effective and sufficiently flexible to identify and target the Army's IT manpower needs. (Because the interviews were limited in scope and involved no original analysis, we cannot conclude one way or the other that the requirements generation process leads to a cost-effective determination of resource requirements, including manpower, or that the process handles the spectrum of future uncertainty in a rigorous fashion.) Second, IT units in the Army are able to meet their recruitment targets and to minimize attrition; however, they struggle somewhat in retaining their personnel. Finally, training and development must be figured into personnel management systems in the future, and their use must be tailored to the Army's particular requirements and needs, as has been the practice.

Air Force Interviews

We learned that Air Force CMF managers for signals occupations (3C series) and intelligence occupations (1N series) face many of the same personnel management issues as Army CMF managers. We also learned that the Air Force has a different requirements generation process and is more severely affected by the long time it takes to obtain a top-secret clearance and by a strenuous operating tempo.

IT Manpower in the Future Force: Requirements Generation Process

Although the actual requirements generation process is much the same in the Air Force as it is in the Army, each service has its own procedures to assess its training and accession needs. As in the Army, the Air Force process for generating requirements focuses on identifying force structure or equipment changes as well as other factors that could alter the required skills or could require a change in the personnel structure. Signal CMF managers explained that education and training requirements were developed in concert with the Air Education and Training Command (AETC) and from information obtained from the field. The CMF manager typically assembles specific requirements in response to information obtained from the consumer communities. The CMF manager presents the requirements to AETC for evaluation. The main arena for this process is the U&TW. Here, participants consider the overall subject matter expertise required by the AFSC, its future manning requirements, and factors or changes that might affect the expertise and manpower that will be needed for an effective future force.

Changes in operating systems are vetted through the U&TW process. The Air Force Communications Agency typically provides input on decisions to upgrade or to change operating systems and on the determination of training needed to support such changes. Operating system changes require new licensing, new software, new training, and equipment upgrades. The step-by-step process used means that changes occur through a graduated response and at a slower pace than in the private sector. However, interviewees said it was not necessary or feasible for the Air Force to adopt changes at the same rate as the private sector.

In addition to its internal systems assessment, the Air Force seeks feedback from the communities employing the airmen trained through Air Force programs and from the airmen themselves. For example, the airmen are surveyed on whether their training was appropriate and adequate for their duties, and the supervisors are required to fill out the Graduate Assessment Survey, which reports on the performance and quality of the airmen and, indirectly, on the effectiveness of the training programs.

In contrast to the quarterly CMF review in the Army, the Air Force U&TW occurs "as needed." This is typically a two-year time cycle in signals occupations. But often more than two years will pass before a U&TW is convened, depending on the magnitude of the changes discussed at the preceding U&TW and the timelines for implementing programs. Clearly, in an IT-intensive field such as signals, systems and technologies can undergo significant change and obsolescence within two years. Given the sheer magnitude of the tasks faced by the U&TW, some difficulty in keeping up with technology is inevitable. However, two years may be too long between reviews in IT.

Assessing the Overall Health of the Unit: Recruitment and Retention

In speaking with Air Force CMF managers, we learned that the two most pervasive problems facing IT personnel management and retention were the long top-secret clearance processing time and the high operational tempo. The length of the top-secret clearance process complicated the training and assignment of qualified IT personnel by preventing trained individuals from beginning or completing their jobs. Although the paperwork for the clearance process started at the schoolhouse, it invariably finished at the assignment over a year later. In many cases, personnel arrive at a billet without their clearance, and for a large portion of their time in billet, they work on tasks that do not require the clearance. When cleared, they may soon be sent to their next assignment, not having done the job for which they were trained and hence with limited preparation for their next job. Airmen denied a clearance must be reclassified. Consequently, Air Force CMF managers stressed that recruiters must do a specific screening for occupations coded as sensitive, to minimize the odds of recruiting someone who ultimately will not be cleared.

Air Force intelligence specialists were also difficult to retain because of their high operational tempo and length of deployment. These factors often deterred intelligence specialists, particularly image analysts and linguists, from continuing their service.

Reclassification was not seen as offering a significant means of improving retention. Because the intelligence career fields were always "chronic/critical," the Air Force allowed airmen to reclassify into intelligence but controlled the grade for reclassification. The preferred threshold for reclassification was E-5, for example.

Recruitment and Retention: Incentives for Enlistment and Reenlistment

As in the Army, the Air Force interviewees reported that reenlistment bonuses were an important retention tool in the signals and intelligence specialties. In fact, the reenlistment bonuses in the signals specialties were among the highest in the Air Force, ranging up to $35,000–40,000, depending on base pay and length of reenlistment. Intelligence specialties, where retention was a chronic problem, also had reenlistment bonuses.

Although reenlistment bonuses have proven effective in reducing the loss of midcareer personnel, they did not reach into the years of service just before retirement eligibility. For example, interviewees were concerned about the lack of reenlistment bonuses after 16 years of service, noting that even the draw of retirement benefits was not sufficient, in some cases, to ensure reenlistment. Those most directly affected by this limit appear to have been the technical master sergeants, whose expertise and experience would be extremely difficult to replace. Furthermore, many CMF managers noted that the enlistment bonuses could be bested by private-sector offers.[9]

Personnel Management and Retention: Incentives for Education and Training

In exploring education and training opportunities in the Air Force, our interviews suggested that the Air Force's career development system is made effective by its multi-tiered structure, which includes both theoretical and hands-on training. The first level of training is the formal aspect, imparted through scheduled on-base schooling required for promotion and for the occupational requirements of specific billets. The second level is on-the-job training and career development, which augment the formal training programs. However, interviewees also reported that the value of the programs as incentives is limited by the difficulty airmen have in actually enrolling in certain courses and by the lack of special pay upon completing the courses.

Training programs in the Air Force take a variety of forms. For example, several programs use mobile training teams with four instructors and that can teach up to 12 students at a time. The mobile training teams provide refresher courses as well as training for new systems. In addition, the Air Force has a surge capacity to escalate the training tempo if needed. During the air operations in Kosovo, for example, the Air Force introduced a theater-deployable communications set, which airmen and members of the Air National Guard had to know how operate prior to deployment. Within six weeks, the Air Force had the equipment and the instructors in place for training, and all deploying personnel were trained before departing for Kosovo.

As in the Army, skill certification in the Air Force was described as an important education/training issue. Interviewees reported that the Air Force generally did not pay for skill certification through Air Force funds. However, there was ongoing work to establish more sophisticated training programs. For example, for signals specialties, a structured on-the-job training program was being developed at Scott Air Force Base. The program would utilize a contractor to provide training for a variety of commercial applications. The contractor would provide airmen who completed the course with a voucher for certification. It was anticipated that this program would be available for a limited number of airmen. Even though certification would have tremendous value to these airmen, interviewees said that the airmen would not incur an additional service obligation unless the courses were more than 20 weeks long.

However, like their counterparts in the Army, Air Force CMF managers said that skill certification brings with it the issue of contractor poaching of qualified airmen. Poach-

---

[9] Some progress has been made toward addressing this problem for officers through the implementation of a Critical Skills Retention Bonus (CSRB) program. This bonus was introduced in the FY01 National Defense Authorization Act. The CSRB program applies to five "critical specialties," including developmental engineering, science, acquisition program management, communications-information systems, and civil engineering. These five career fields were chosen because of their importance to mission completion and their relatively low retention rates. The bonus applies to officers with between four and thirteen years of commissioned service and offers them a bonus of $10,000 per year for committing to an additional four-year contract. This program demonstrates the recognition among defense officials of the need to offer larger reenlistment incentives in critical career fields. The Air Force has been relatively more active than the other services in its use of this bonus program (see Banda, 2002).

ing occurs actively and passively. Even if there was no direct pitch, the airmen could easily observe that the instructor was more highly compensated, had a more flexible work schedule and workplace environment, and had significantly fewer responsibilities.

Although the training opportunities for Air Force intelligence specialties appear extensive, interviewees also reported that training courses were not accessible enough to allow them to contribute centrally to personnel development. Intelligence specialties have many classes available to airmen who want to acquire additional skills. For the most part, initial training for Air Force intelligence specialties occurs at Goodfellow Air Force Base. There are also some joint training opportunities at Ft. Huachuca and language training at the Language School in Monterey. Some courses are considered in promotion decisions, such as the advanced signal analysis course. There are also opportunities for a three-year internship at the Defense Intelligence Agency, but this is a highly competitive opportunity and requires a three-year commitment.

There appear to be several obstacles that prevent airmen from pursuing higher training. For example, we were told that the Air Force rarely let airmen attend these classes because of critical manning shortfalls in this area. Furthermore, Air Force intelligence CMF managers indicated that airmen who acquire specialized training, such as those who go through the joint imagery analyst course, could in some cases become a problem to manage because they are so specialized.

As in the Army, the Air Force uses incentives to induce airmen to seek further training. For example, there are incentives to reclassify into signals specialties. According to one CMF manager, reclassifications into signals rose during the economic boom in part because of the perception that these specialties paid more in the private sector. The same CMF manager also noted that reclassification into the signals AFSC is a means of obtaining soldiers from other services who are exhausted by the PERSTEMPO or OPTEMPO of their originating service. Thus, this CMF manager suggested that the lifestyle of the Air Force signals career field was an attractive occupation for some soldiers.

Promotion is another means of rewarding and managing intelligence personnel. Because intelligence specialties are on the list of "chronic/critical" specialties, they promote more quickly than other career fields. This can encourage potential recruits to enter IT and intelligence fields. However, obtaining a promotion requires considerable effort. Promotions are based on competitive test scores, and many test takers in intelligence have college degrees.

The Air Force has also made significant use of the Information Assurance Scholarship Program (IASP). This scholarship is offered to individuals pursuing a bachelors, masters, or doctoral degree in information assurance disciplines. To be eligible, an individual must be at least a junior at a designated Center for Academic Excellence (CAE) and must maintain a sufficient grade point average. Military personnel and civilian DoD employees are also eligible for the scholarship. IASP students begin their studies at the Information Resources Management College at National Defense University and then transfer to another CAE, the Air Force Institute of Technology, or the Naval Postgraduate School. By accepting the scholarship, recipients agree to serve a period of obligated service (one year for each academic year of scholarship) in a DoD information assurance position.[10] IASP gives individuals an incentive to earn a degree in IT-related fields and ensures the services a steady inflow of trained personnel.

---

[10] *Information Assurance Scholarship Program: Program Overview,* www.denfselink.mil/nii/iasp, accessed November 2003.

While some incentives encourage personnel to seek additional training, interviewees said that the absence of special pay and the lack of a link between additional skills and enhanced military career opportunities somewhat limit the appeal of the training and development program to airmen. Some of these limits reflect the fact that the services base their training quotas on the skills required to fill specific job requirements and do not fund the explicit use of training as a retention tool. CMF managers said there is no special pay for acquiring additional training, excepting foreign language proficiency pay ($100 to $300 per month), which is given to airmen who learn another language and maintain their skill level in it. In addition, there is also special duty assignment pay for human intelligence occupations, including debriefers, but these are low-density occupations (there are 48 such occupations in the Air Force). However, our interviews and research suggest that perhaps a more direct use of training as a retention tool might be an effective use of funds.

But while interviewees noted that some IT personnel used opportunities gained in the Air Force to seek private-sector employment, the CMF managers who we spoke with also noted that some airmen who leave in pursuit of high pay in the private sector ultimately fail to find it and return to the Air Force. Our interviewees said that such individuals are "object lessons" to others considering such moves.

The incentive to seek additional training is sometimes also undermined by the fact that acquiring additional skills does not increase the variety of assignments available to the airman. The Air Force primarily uses move-eligibility rules rather than qualifications to sort airmen into assignments. For example, time in station is a factor affecting assignment eligibility. This is quite different from the Army, where acquiring new skills can increase the choice of future assignments.

Key Issues

Our interviews with Air Force career field managers offer similar insights into IT personnel training and management as found in our Army interviews. First, the Air Force has a well-defined process for generating resource requirements including manpower requirements. Furthermore, the Air Force has a variety of training programs and incentives intended to recruit and retain personnel, as well as to prepare airmen for future challenges. However, our interviews also indicated that training courses were often not easily accessible and that the IT personnel management system lacked direct incentives for airmen who take additional training, such as special pay or particular career opportunities. Finally, as we discovered in our Army interviews, it appears that retention is the most significant problem faced by the military's IT sector. The Air Force addresses this issue with reenlistment bonuses, but some interviewees felt that the use of bonuses should extend into years of service 15 to 20 in order to increase the ability to maintain an experienced IT workforce.

Observations and Conclusions

Although our interviews were limited in their scope, we offer some preliminary conclusions from our discussion of them. First, both the Army and the Air Force have processes in place to determine future manning and training requirements over the near term. In the case of new systems or hardware, this typically means a four-year or longer cycle of planning and procurement. We did not learn whether the fast pace of change in IT has resulted in more rapid procurement or has overstressed the requirement determination processes. Still, the interviews suggest that the requirements generation processes can be speeded up when necessary (by holding meetings or reviews more frequently); hence the processes have a capacity for responding to changing circumstances or opportunities. (The Army CMF review occurred on a quarterly basis, while the Structure Manning Decision Review was on a two-year-or-less cycle but could be accelerated.) Such responsiveness is similar to the flexibility that we referred to at the start of this chapter, where we argued that a flexible, adaptive process was more important than seemingly precise estimates of distant requirements. The use of mobile training teams, commercial training programs, and adapted bonus incentives are examples of the ways that the current planning procedures exhibit their responsiveness and their ability to prepare IT personnel for the changing nature of military affairs.

Interviewees in both services reported difficulty retaining IT personnel. We understood that the value of IT and other technical skills in the private sector helped attract personnel into these specialties. But once personnel had been trained and gained experience, their private-sector opportunities were tangible and alluring. Skill certification programs and poaching by contractors who provide training were variants on this theme. The military provided skills; skill certification made them more easily transferable to the private sector, and civilian trainers pipelined information about outside pay and job opportunities to trainees. The verdict was out on whether programs offering certification had at the same time been able to maintain or increase retention (e.g., the Army's Cisco Routers Certification program). Our interviews also found that within both the Army and the Air Force, there was no skill-based special pay for IT or MI personnel to encourage them to obtain additional training and remain in the military (with the exception of language-related special pay).

Although in some cases IT occupations had lower retention rates than the average, the flavor of the interviews was that while IT retention was a significant challenge, it was a challenge that could be met. Reenlistment bonuses, faster promotion, greater choice in assignments, access to the latest IT hardware and software, and ample, accessible training opportunities are all retention tools. Bonuses have been used most extensively, and the other tools could be developed further than their role in the past. Furthermore, the interviews revealed that the services were well aware of the importance of IT in military capability and were taking steps to modernize their equipment and train their personnel more effectively. This trend presumably adds to the attractiveness of military IT positions.

Finally, as was suggested in previous chapters, the importance of training and education in attracting motivated recruits and retaining key personnel was consistently stressed in our interviews. This supports the overall argument of this report, that the training offered in military IT occupations and its civilian sector value are core factors in determining the supply of IT personnel and helping the services meet their IT manpower requirements.

The following chapters will discuss this hypothesis more completely, outlining actual data on IT personnel flows in the services and using a theoretical model to demonstrate the intentions and effects of the incentives and retention tools described above.

CHAPTER FOUR

Evidence on Enlisted Personnel Flows in IT Occupations

In this chapter, we ask whether military IT occupations had poorer supply outcomes than did non-IT occupations during a period including the economic boom and dot-com bubble of the 1990s. The runaway demand for IT workers in the private sector could be expected to hurt the military's efforts to attract and keep IT personnel, and if so, it would not be surprising to find lower recruit quality and lower retention in IT than non-IT. Furthermore, although the military had tools such as advertising, enlistment bonuses, and recruiting resources to compete with the private sector, these tools might not have been an adequate counterpoint. To determine how well military IT personnel supply fared compared with non-IT personnel supply, we analyzed data on recruit quality, term length, attrition, and first-term reenlistment. Our analysis is descriptive. It does not identify the specific effect of variables such as bonuses, unemployment, military/civilian pay, or recruiters on personnel supply, but it does reveal whether IT supply outcomes were worse, the same, or better than those of non-IT.

We present charts contrasting IT and non-IT supply outcomes and predictions of the outcomes with respect to Armed Forces Qualification Test (AFQT) score category, a measure of personnel quality. The predictions are based on regressions reported in Appendix A.[1] By studying the results of these comparisons, we can conclude that the IT field has several qualities that assist it in attracting high-quality recruits into IT and which might or might not assist in retaining IT personnel beyond the first term of service. Most important among these qualities appears to be the perceived value of the IT training and the willingness of high-quality recruits to enlist in order to receive this training.

Preview of Findings

Contrary to popular expectations, we conclude from our research that IT occupations attracted higher-quality recruits, had lower attrition, and often had a longer enlistment term than did non-IT occupations. Higher quality and longer terms speak to the attractiveness of IT occupations for recruits and to the services' commitment to man IT positions to a high level of proficiency. Lower attrition in IT is partly a consequence of higher quality recruits. As previous research has shown, high-quality recruits are more likely to complete basic and advanced training and to stay for the duration of their terms. But attrition is lower in IT

[1] Tables A.9–A.12 contain regression results and hypothesis tests.

even after controlling for quality. The lower attrition may reflect the value of remaining in the military to acquire IT training.

In the previous chapter, our interviews suggested the difficulty of retaining IT personnel once they had been trained. However, despite this anecdotal evidence, actual personnel flows show that IT occupations do not have significantly worse retention than do non-IT occupations. In fact, the difference in reenlistment between IT and non-IT occupations is small. IT reenlistment is lower than non-IT reenlistment in the Army and Navy, but IT and non-IT reenlistment are the same in the Air Force, and IT reenlistment is slightly higher in the Marine Corps. We also find that for high-aptitude personnel, reenlistment is lower in the Army and Air Force but higher in the Navy and Marine Corps.

Our comparisons also reveal differences in personnel management practices by service. For instance, the Air Force and Marine Corps had low attrition for personnel entering in FYs 1993–1998; the Navy had mid-level, declining attrition; and the Army had high and rising attrition. Also, reenlistment rates differed by service—first-term reenlistment was highest in the Air Force, somewhat lower in the Army and the Navy, and lowest in the Marine Corps. Reenlistment was low in the Marine Corps by design. The Marine Corps prefers a predominately junior personnel force structure, and putting a large first-term force next to a small career force means that first-term Marines must vie for relatively few second-term positions. In our data window for reenlistment decisions, FYs 1997–2001, the Marine Corps reenlistment rate was about 24 percent, while Army and Navy rates were 45–50 percent and the Air Force rate was around 55 percent.

Defining the Occupational Groups

As discussed in Chapter Two, we distinguish between IT-core, IT-related, and non-IT occupations. The IT-core occupations are those designated as information technology or information assurance occupations in the Pentagon's report (U.S. Office of the Secretary of Defense, 1999). IT-related occupations are those that rely extensively on IT in duty performance; these have been selected using the best judgment of the authors. Prominent among IT-related occupations are detection, surveillance, control, and intelligence functions. Non-IT occupations are those in which IT is not involved or plays a lesser role. Table 4.1 (which is identical to Table 2.2) provides the IT-core and IT-related occupations and gives examples of non-IT occupations.

Means

We begin with a simple table of means.[2] The table of means and much of the other data analysis in this chapter are based on the PERSTEMPO file. The means reveal the main differences in the outcomes for IT and non-IT occupations and in the aptitudes, education,

[2] The PERSTEMPO file is used throughout this chapter. The Defense Manpower Data Center created this file from active duty enlisted and officer personnel and pay records. The file is a longitudinal file of individuals. For a more complete description of the file, see Hosek and Totten (1998, 2002).

Table 4.1
IT-Core, IT-Related, and Examples of Other (Non-IT) Military Occupations

IT Core	IT Related	Examples of Non-IT
Information system operator	Navigator	Tracked vehicle maintenance
Telecommunication computer maintainer	Radar, sonar operator	Missile mechanic
Network analyst	Surveillance	Construction
Small computer system specialist	Fire control	Aircraft engine maintenance
Information management	Missile guidance control	Supply administration
Radio communication systems	Electronic countermeasures	Nuclear, biological, chemical warfare
Automated data processing repair	Operational intelligence	Medical, dental
	Mapping	Language interpretation
	Auditing	Security guard
	Precision equipment	Infantry, armor, artillery
		Air crew

gender, and race/ethnicity composition for members of these occupations. We present means for IT and non-IT occupations, by service, for the percentage of recruits who are high quality, the percentage selecting a long initial term, the percentage not completing at least three years of a four-year term, and the percentage reenlisting given that they completed a four-year term (Table 4.2). IT occupations include both IT-related and IT-core occupations, which are combined because of the similarity in their means. We also present means for the percentage in each AFQT category, non–high school graduate (non-HSG), general equivalency diploma (GED), female, black, and Hispanic.

Two differences stand out. First, in every service the percentage of recruits who are high quality is much higher in IT than in non-IT. High-quality recruits are defined as those who have a high school diploma and an AFQT score at the 50th percentile or above. Second, IT occupations are much more likely than non-IT occupations to have recruits who score in the top AFQT percentiles, namely, AFQT categories I and II.[3] In the Air Force, for instance, 40 percent of the recruits in non-IT are in categories I–II, compared with 68 percent of the recruits in IT.

Our results also demonstrate important differences between IT and non-IT occupations with respect to length of term, attrition, and reenlistment rates. Recruits select a longer term in IT than in non-IT in the Army and Marine Corps, while there is little difference in term length in the Navy and Air Force. In addition, attrition, computed for members with a four-year term of enlistment,[4] is more than a third lower in IT than in non-IT in the Navy, the Marine Corps, and the Air Force, and a few percentage points lower in the Army. Finally, reenlistment rates are lower in IT than in non-IT in the Army and the Navy, the same in the Air Force, and slightly higher in IT in the Marine Corps.

[3] The mapping of AFQT categories to AFQT percentiles is as follows: category I–II, 65 and above; IIIA, 50–64; IIIB, 31–49; IV, 10–30. Category V's are not accessed, and as Table 4.2 shows, very few category IVs are accessed.

[4] In our attrition and reenlistment regressions, we include personnel with term lengths of three, four, five, and six years.

Table 4.2
Means for IT and Non-IT Occupations by Service (percentage)

	Army		Navy		Marine Corps		Air Force	
Variable	**Non-IT**	**IT**	**Non-IT**	**IT**	**Non-IT**	**IT**	**Non-IT**	**IT**
High quality	42	56	52	68	56	77	70	86
Long term	11	19	7	7	10	36	18	20
Attrition	29	26	28	21	23	14	21	14
Reenlist	49	45	48	45	23	25	56	56
AFQT I–II	30	51	35	53	32	58	40	68
AFQT IIIA	28	27	24	24	27	22	32	20
AFQT IIIB	35	17	35	18	36	16	24	10
AFQT IV–V	2	1	0	0	1	0	0	0
Non-HSG	4	4	6	4	5	3	4	3
GED	8	8	2	3	0	0	0	0
Some college	5	5	7	7	5	4	1	1
Female	2	3	2	1	1	1	11	16
Black	19	17	18	14	6	7	23	30
Hispanic	25	21	20	16	13	14	17	16

NOTE: High quality = high school graduate and AFQT score of 50 or higher. Long term = initial term length of five or six years. Attrition = completed fewer than three years of a four-year term. Reenlist = for members with a four-year term of service, we defined reenlistment by the condition that the member is present in the data file 3 months before and 12 months after his expiration of term of service (ETS) date. AFQT "unknown" is omitted. If included, AFQT percentages sum to 100.

In other areas, differences between IT and non-IT occupations are negligible. For example, the compositions of IT and non-IT occupations appear to be virtually the same in terms of non–high school graduate, GED, and some college. Differences in percentage female are minor also, except that the Air Force percentage female is higher in IT than in non-IT. Race/ethnic differences vary by service. The Army and the Navy have lower percentages of blacks and Hispanics in IT, whereas the Marine Corps has practically no difference and the Air Force has a higher percentage of blacks in IT than in non-IT.

Number and Quality of Entrants into IT Positions

To begin, we look at the number of entrants into IT occupations compared with non-IT occupations. We measure the number of entrants into IT occupations by the number of first-year enlisted personnel in an IT occupation, using the classification in Table 4.1. This provides a good overall measure of the demand for new IT personnel,[5] and in the military's port-of-entry labor system the new entrants form the pool of future leaders and experienced personnel. We find that in recent years about one in five enlisted entrants are in IT-core or IT-related occupations, i.e., about 30,000 of 150,000 (Table 4.3).

[5] The count of new entrants in IT has some limitations as a measure of the demand for new IT personnel. It assumes that the services were able to enlist enough personnel into IT to meet their demand, and it uses the occupational code attached to the member's personnel record in the first year (some personnel might not yet have an occupational code). We use DoD occupational coding, and these codes have been stable over time.

Table 4.3
First-Year Enlisted Personnel by Occupational Group, 1978–2001

Year	IT Core	IT Related	Non-IT	Total	% IT Core	% IT Related	% Non-IT
1978	22,374	31,782	181,395	235,551	9.5	13.5	77.0
1979	22,717	34,453	185,048	242,218	9.4	14.2	76.4
1980	22,248	43,427	211,523	277,198	8.0	15.7	76.3
1981	20,108	43,932	192,904	256,944	7.8	17.1	75.1
1982	22,262	40,444	175,046	237,752	9.4	17.0	73.6
1983	23,025	36,840	179,928	239,793	9.6	15.4	75.0
1984	19,590	38,553	185,907	244,050	8.0	15.8	76.2
1985	17,159	37,984	183,197	238,340	7.2	15.9	76.9
1986	17,953	42,825	187,417	248,195	7.2	17.3	75.5
1987	13,826	42,960	180,775	237,561	5.8	18.1	76.1
1988	13,386	42,821	160,319	216,526	6.2	19.8	74.0
1989	14,018	46,208	159,885	220,111	6.4	21.0	72.6
1990	11,258	35,117	131,590	177,965	6.3	19.7	73.9
1991	9,945	29,932	116,611	156,488	6.4	19.1	74.5
1992	9,839	24,899	122,903	157,641	6.2	15.8	78.0
1993	7,879	18,401	86,196	112,569	7.0	16.3	76.6
1994	7,650	20,125	110,860	138,729	5.5	14.5	79.9
1995	8,292	20,349	108,377	137,018	6.1	14.9	79.1
1996	9,051	24,820	113,824	147,695	6.1	16.8	77.1
1997	9,930	21,460	121,483	152,873	6.5	14.0	79.5
1998	8,799	20,035	123,253	152,087	5.8	13.2	81.0
1999	10,199	21,584	122,372	154,155	6.6	14.0	79.4
2000	10,173	24,276	130,709	165,158	6.2	14.7	79.1
2001	7,987	19,394	124,441	151,822	5.3	12.8	82.0

SOURCES: Authors' tabulations from files provided by the Defense Manpower Data Center (DMDC). Tabulations for 1978–1992 are from the DMDC Special Cohort Accession and Continuer (DSCAC) file, and tabulations for 1993–2001 are from the PERSTEMPO file. The DSCAC file is a longitudinal file created by the DMDC of enlisted members based on their personnel records. The occupation code used in creating this table is the DoD occupational code appearing on the individual's record. An occupation is typically assigned after a recruit has successfully completed advanced individual training. In occupations requiring long training, this may be in the second year of service. Also, in the Navy some sailors may begin as "general detail" and only subsequently qualify to train in a particular occupation.

The percentage of first-year personnel in IT has declined slightly over the period 1978–2001. In the 1980s, nearly 25 percent of enlisted entrants were in IT-core or IT-related occupations. There are several possible causes of the relative decrease in IT positions. It may be that despite the extensive increase in the military's use of IT, the productivity of IT systems and software has led to labor saving, so that IT tasks can be done by fewer personnel. Also, some IT slots may have been outsourced to civilian contractors, and some IT specialties may have been reclassified as non-IT.

The drop in the absolute number of IT entrants in the early 1990s resulted from the draw down. Non-IT slots were also cut, so there was little change in the percentage of entrants in IT. In addition, year-to-year variation in the number of IT entrants probably reflects the adjustment of accession targets in response to higher- or lower-than-expected retention. In an unexpectedly good year for retention, for instance, accession targets are reduced.

Because the performance achieved by IT systems depends on personnel quality, the quality of recruits in this field is as important as their number. Our research on this issue reveals that in each service and in each year that we looked at, the percentage of high-quality recruits is higher in IT than in non-IT. Because approximately 90 percent of Army, Navy, and Marine Corps recruits are high school graduates, as are nearly 99 percent of Air Force recruits, almost all of the difference between occupational groups in the percentage of those who are high quality comes from the AFQT score. It is clear that high-scoring recruits are willing to enter IT, and the services are willing to let them enter rather than redirecting them to another occupational area.

Figure 4.1 displays the percentage of first-year personnel who are high quality, grouped by non-IT, IT-related, and IT-core occupations.[6,7] These graphs support the observation above that for each year and each service, the percentage of high-quality recruits is higher in IT than in non-IT.

The graphs also suggest that the percentage of high-quality recruits in a service varies from year to year. Previous analyses of the supply of high-quality recruits suggest that these variations depend on recruiting resources (e.g., number of recruiters and number of recruiting stations), recruiter incentives, advertising, educational benefits, enlistment bonuses, military/civilian pay, and the unemployment rate (see Warner, Simon, and Payne, 2001). The draw down in military personnel was still under way in FYs 1993–1995, and during these years the services had a low demand for new recruits. This, plus a soft economy, made it comparatively easy for the percentage of recruits who were high quality to be high. Recruiting conditions worsened in the latter half of the 1990s, and the demand for recruits increased. Unemployment reached a 30-year low, civilian wages rose faster than military pay, and the demand for IT workers boomed. As a result, the services found it much more difficult to maintain a high percentage of high-quality recruits. The Army, Navy, and Air Force were hard pressed to meet even their overall numerical targets for recruits, let alone their targets for high-quality recruits. The Air Force did not make its goal for high-quality recruits in FY 1998, and the Army and the Navy missed their goals in FY 1999 (Asch, Hosek, and Warner, 2001). The Navy and the Marine Corps succeeded in holding the percentage of high-quality recruits steady from FY 1997 to FY 2001, but the Air Force experienced a decline. In response to these recruiting difficulties, in FY 1999 Congress incorporated provisions in the FY 2000 National Defense Authorization Act to increase military pay, enlistment incentives, and advertising. Above-normal pay increases were passed again in FY 2001 in an effort to increase the enlistment of high-quality personnel. The soft economy in 2001–2003 also aided recruiting.[8]

Regardless of these yearly variations, our probit regressions indicate that higher-AFQT recruits are more likely to enter IT. Table 4.4 contains predictions from regressions on whether a recruit entered IT (or not) as a function of AFQT, education, gender, race/ethnicity, and fiscal year.[9] As seen, the probability of entering IT increases with AFQT.

---

[6] The figures and tables in this chapter are based on authors' tabulations from the PERSTEMPO file, unless otherwise stated. The percentage of those who are high quality shown in Figure 4.1 end at FY 2001 because the FY 2002 data appeared anomalous, probably because of lags in reporting and in updating the AFQT score in the PERSTEMPO file.

[7] The plunge in the Army percentage of those who are high quality in FY 1997 in Figure 4.1 is a data problem. Education is coded as missing for 70 percent of first-term members.

[8] For further discussion, see Asch et al. (2002).

[9] The predicted probabilities are for white males. The use of other race/ethnicity characteristics would not change the pattern of AFQT effects on the predicted probability, although the level of the probability would change. This point also applies to subsequent tables with predicted probabilities.

Figure 4.1
Percentage of First-Year Personnel Who Are "High Quality," by Service and IT Group, FYs 1993–2001

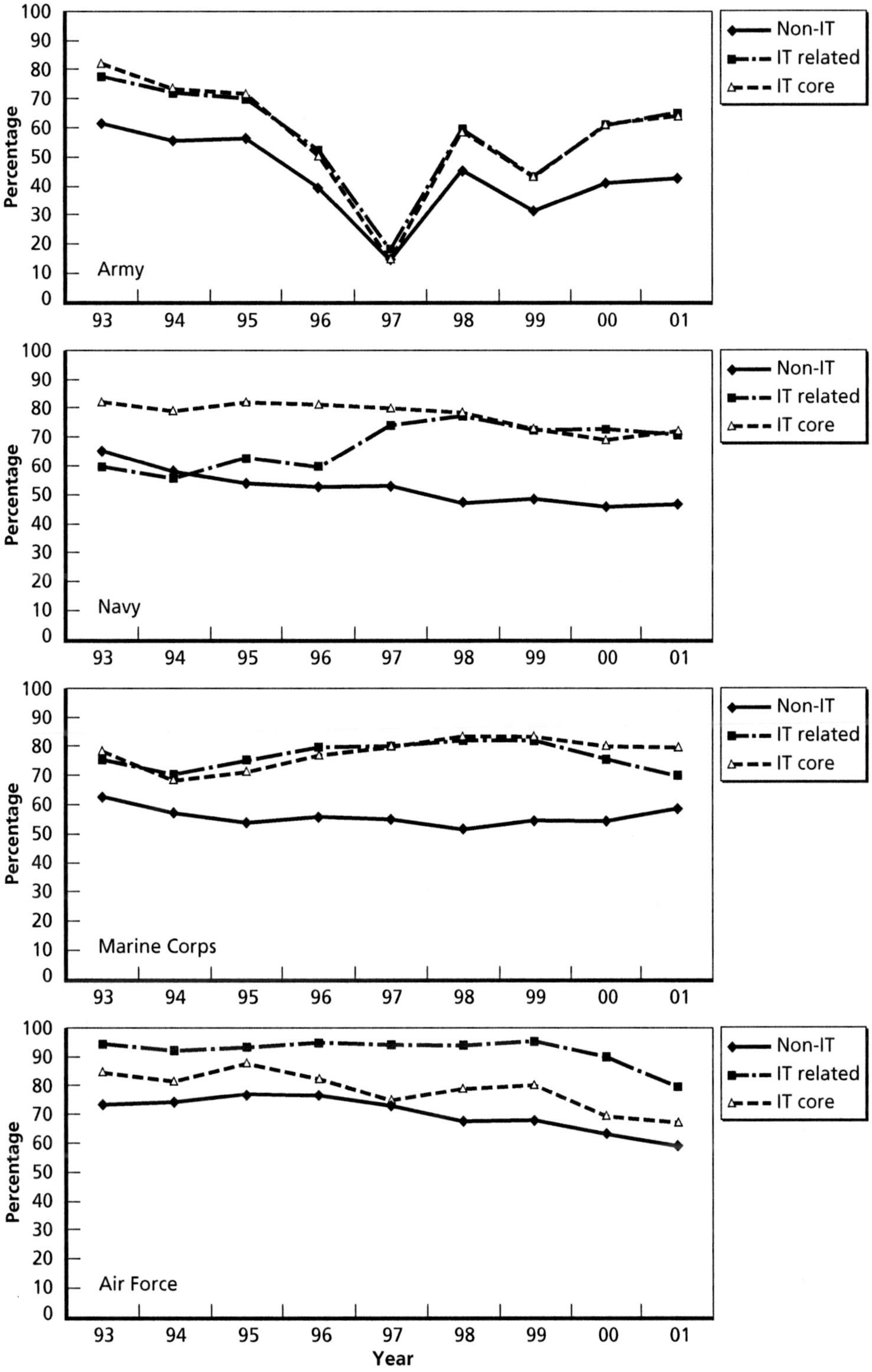

RAND *MG108-4.1*

Table 4.4
Predicted Probability of Entering an IT Occupation, by AFQT Category

Variable	Army	Navy	Marine Corps	Air Force
AFQT I–II	.31	.22	.22	.34
AFQT IIIA	.20	.15	.10	.15
AFQT IIIB	.11	.08	.05	.09

Term Length

While IT occupations are attractive to high-quality recruits, our analysis also suggests that recruits are willing to sign up for longer terms of service in IT occupations than in non-IT. There are several explanations for this observation. A service may be able to capitalize on the relative attractiveness of IT jobs by encouraging recruits who enter IT occupations to select a longer term of service. In addition, training tends to be longer in more technical occupations such as IT, and the services may prefer to offer longer terms to keep the time on duty after training on a par with other occupations, or even longer. Further, enlistment incentives, if offered, are generally larger for longer terms, increasing the payoff to recruits willing to enter IT positions. Longer terms are beneficial for services because they offer a greater return on their investment in recruiting and training, less unit turnover (depending on the rotation policy), and greater proficiency on duty because of greater experience. The advantages are greater if the recruit is high quality. High-quality recruits, as mentioned, have a high success rate in training, less attrition, and high performance on duty.

In Figure 4.2 we see the percentage of first-year enlisted personnel with terms of five or six years. The modal term length in all services is four years. The Army offers a few two-year terms and some three-year terms. In FY 2001, 44 percent of its non-IT terms were three year, as were only 17 percent of IT related and 3 percent of IT core. The Navy offered three-year terms in the mid-1990s, but like the Marine Corps it has offered virtually no two- or three-year terms in recent years. The Air Force offers only four-year or longer terms and in FY 1999 shifted to a policy under which nearly half of its terms were six year.

The figure indicates that since FY 1997, long terms are two to three times more common among IT than non-IT in the Army. About 10 percent of non-IT terms are long versus 20–30 percent of IT terms. In the Navy, fewer than 10 percent of IT and non-IT terms are long, and there is little difference between IT and non-IT term length. With the exception of FY 2001, in the Marine Corps only about 10 percent of non-IT terms were long, compared with 20 percent in IT core and 40–50 percent in IT related. In the Air Force in FYs 1999–2001, around 50 percent of non-IT and IT-related terms were long, as were 35 percent of IT-core terms. All of these were six-year terms.

Our probit regressions on the choice of a longer first term reveal a positive AFQT effect. Enlistment incentives offer a partial explanation for this; they are larger for longer terms. But the explanation is only partial because the incentive amount does not increase with AFQT score. As an additional explanation, the positive relationship between term length and AFQT over the entire range of AFQT suggests that the recruit's perceived value of IT training and experience increases with AFQT. A related, demand-side explanation is

Figure 4.2
Percentage of First-Year Personnel with Initial Term Length of Five or Six Years, by Service and IT Group, FYs 1993–2001

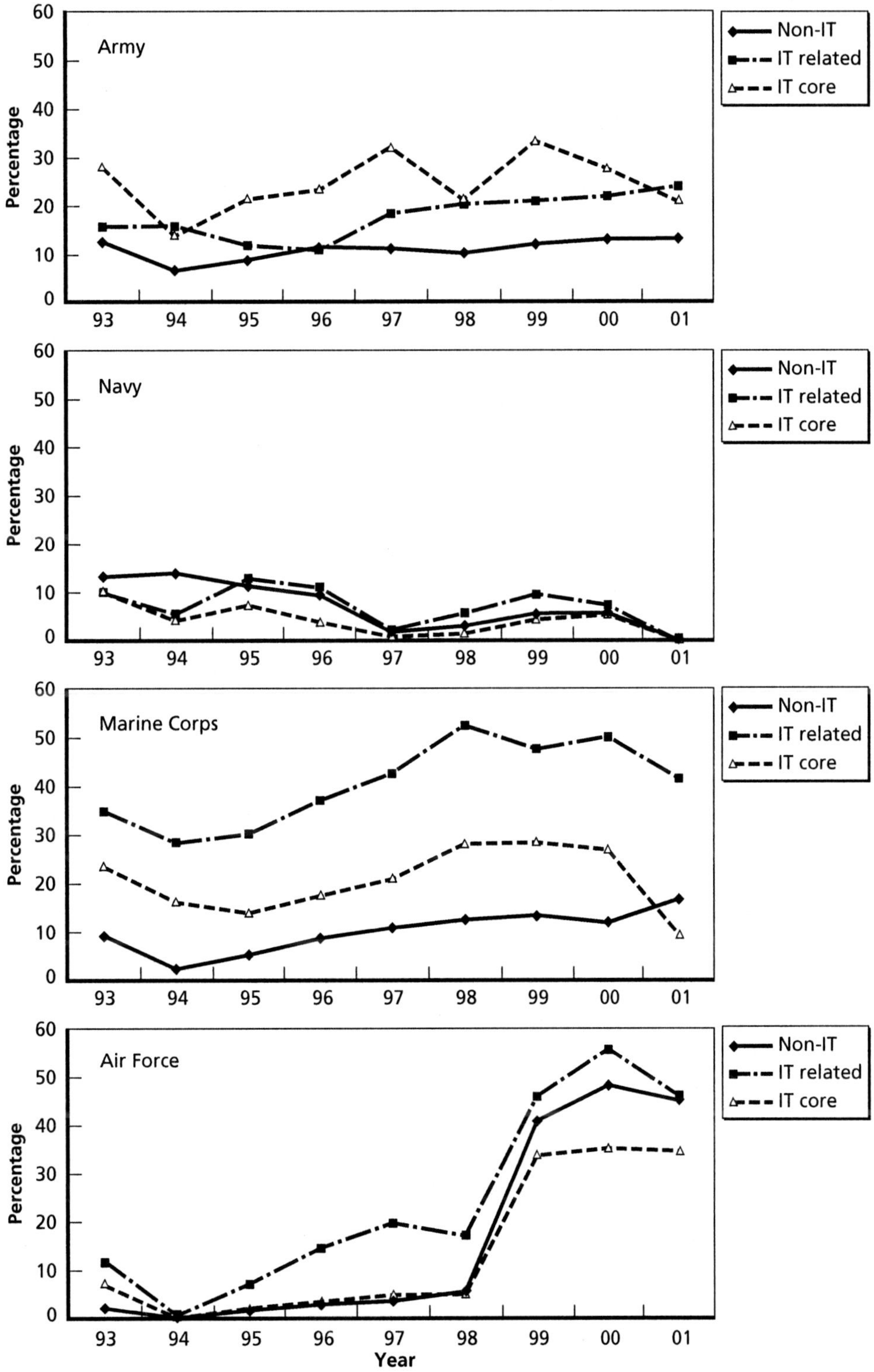

RAND *MG108-4.2*

that a service's process of matching recruits to jobs might ration IT positions to high-AFQT recruits, and the service could ration the number of shorter terms to induce recruits to select a longer term. Recruits with a higher perceived value from IT training would be more likely to accept such an offer, and arguably these recruits would be high AFQT.

To see the effect of AFQT, we computed the probability of selecting a long term by AFQT category (Table 4.5). The probability of choosing a longer term rises with AFQT, supporting the hypothesis that IT training is more valuable for high-quality personnel.

Table 4.5
Predicted Probability of Selecting a Five- or Six-Year First Term in IT and Non-IT Occupations, by AFQT Category

	Army		Navy		Marine Corps		Air Force	
Variable	Non-IT	IT	Non-IT	IT	Non-IT	IT	Non-IT	IT
AFQT I–II	.22	.26	.00	.00	.28	.71	.53	.66
AFQT IIIA	.17	.17	.00	.00	.17	.39	.46	.51
AFQT IIIB	.08	.09	.00	.00	.07	.08	.42	.25

NOTE: Navy probabilities reflect this service's infrequent use of long terms.

Attrition

Our analysis demonstrates that not only do IT occupations attract more highly qualified personnel who select longer terms, but they also have lower attrition than non-IT occupations. This was clearly evident for the Navy, Air Force, and Marine Corps, though less so for the Army (Figure 4.3). Navy, Marine Corps, and Air Force IT attrition was about 10 points lower (over a third lower) than non-IT attrition, and Army attrition was a few points lower. The figure shows the percentage of members who entered service in a given fiscal year with a four-year term and completed fewer than three years of the term. The figure ends at the FY 1998 cohort of entrants because following them for three years to FY 2001 brought us to the end of our data window. During the period shown, Army attrition was high and rising, reflecting a severe challenge in controlling personnel outflow. Two of five members of the Army's FY 1998 cohort did not finish their four-year term, and IT attrition was only slightly lower than non-IT attrition. Navy IT-core attrition was about 10 points lower than non-IT, and IT-related attrition declined to equal that of IT core. Marine Corps attrition was about 25 percent for non-IT and 15 percent for IT. Air Force attrition was about 22 percent for non-IT and 13 percent for IT.

Focusing on the effect of AFQT, Table 4.6 presents the predicted probability of attrition within two years of service with respect to AFQT category. The regression variables include AFQT category, education, race/ethnicity, fiscal year, and term length. We see that attrition is somewhat lower as AFQT rises, but the major difference is that in any AFQT category, attrition is lower in IT than in non-IT. In nearly every case, this difference is statistically significant.

Figure 4.3
Cumulative Attrition at Three-Year Point for Four-Year Enlistees Entering in FYs 1993–1998, by Service and IT Group

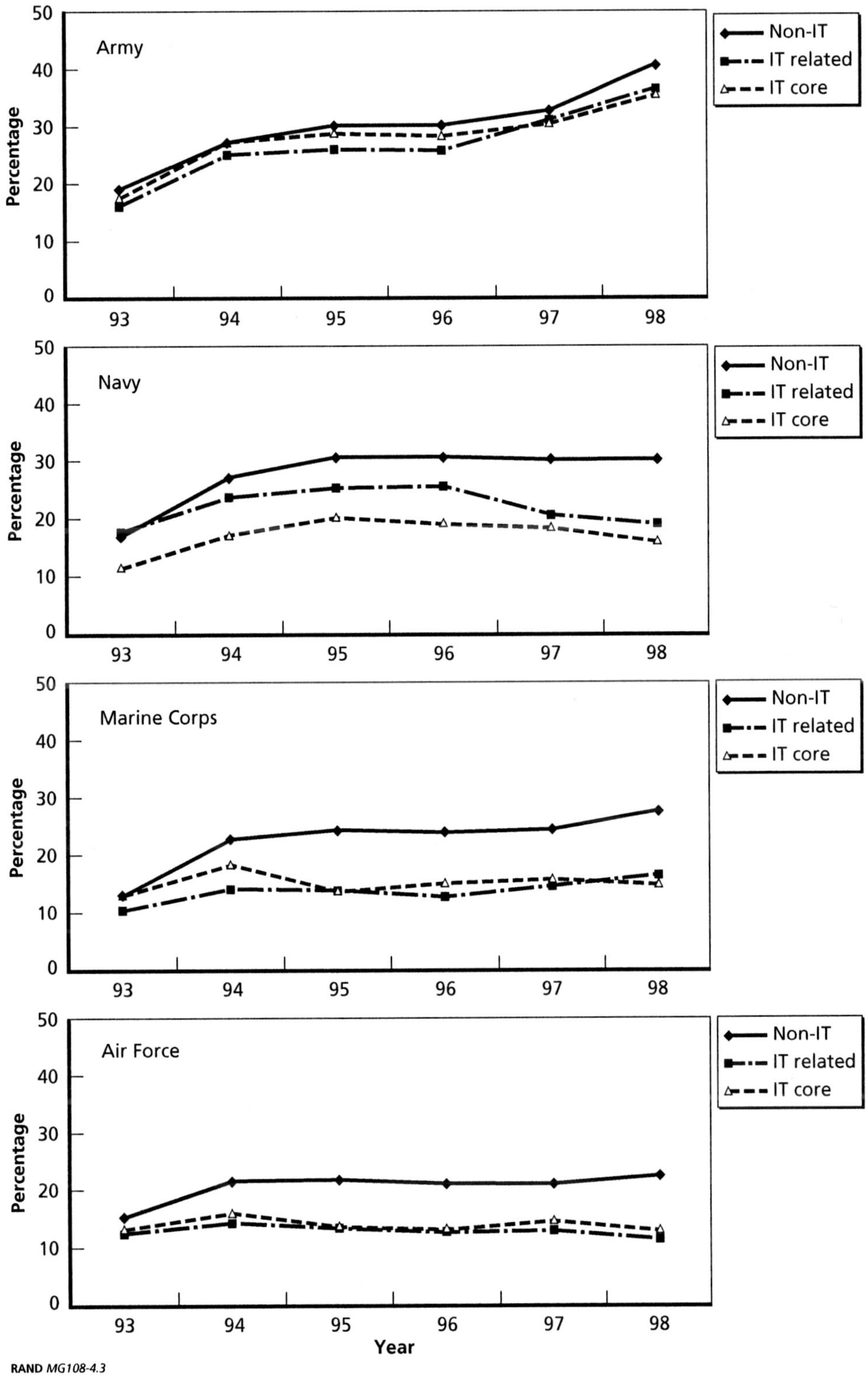

RAND *MG108-4.3*

Table 4.6
Predicted Probability of Two-Year Attrition in IT and Non-IT Occupations, by AFQT Category

	Army		Navy		Marine Corps		Air Force	
Variable	Non-IT	IT	Non-IT	IT	Non-IT	IT	Non-IT	IT
AFQT I–II	.18	.17	.17	.12	.15	.04	.12	.08
AFQT IIIA	.21	.20	.18	.14	.16	.06	.13	.03
AFQT IIIB	.21	.20	.19	.15	.17	.08	.14	.06

By implication, the lower IT attrition seen in Figure 4.3 occurs not only because attrition tends to decline with AFQT and IT has more high-AFQT members than non-IT, but also because the effect of AFQT on attrition in IT is "more negative." This is consistent with the idea that the value of training motivates IT personnel to complete their terms and, further, that the value of training is higher for high-AFQT personnel.

Reenlistment

A final area of comparison between IT and non-IT occupations is that of reenlistment rates.[10] While we expected to find that IT occupations had more difficulty retaining trained personnel given the private-sector compensation in IT jobs, our results suggest instead that the reenlistment rates were similar for IT and non-IT occupations over FYs 1997–2001, the period of boom and bust for IT careers. Thus, even though IT occupations might have had a lower latent reenlistment rate, the policies pursued by the services apparently kept IT reenlistment close to non-IT reenlistment. Figure 4.4 shows the similarity in IT and non-IT reenlistment rates, and in some cases IT rates are higher than non-IT rates. The figure is based on personnel with a four-year term of service.

What factors might affect reenlistment in addition to outside wage and employment opportunities? Previous research has shown a small effect of AFQT on reenlistment; so despite the difference in AFQT between IT and non-IT occupations, we would not expect much difference in reenlistment from AFQT.[11] Attrition and bonuses are also factors to consider. Attrition presumably removes members least likely to reenlist, and attrition rates are higher in non-IT than in IT occupations. Therefore, the difference in attrition should increase reenlistment in non-IT relative to that in IT. Furthermore, reenlistment bonuses serve to shore up reenlistment rates. Bonuses could increase reenlistment in either IT or non-IT depending on the extent and level of bonuses applied to each. In Chapter Five, we report some evidence of greater bonus usage and higher amounts in IT. The expected value of ad-

---

[10] We defined reenlistment by the condition that the member is present 3 months before and 12 months after his ETS date. We did not control for whether a person was eligible to reenlist; our data do not contain this information. For four-year enlistees, the data series begins with FY 1997 because the initial ETS is picked up from the FY 1993 record.

[11] See Hosek and Mattock (2003) for instance. However, as seen, AFQT also reduces attrition somewhat. Therefore, more high-AFQT personnel complete their terms and reach the reenlistment point. Cooke and Quester (1992) actually found that, when measured in terms of entry cohort, reenlistment of higher-aptitude personnel is higher. This is because their attrition is lower, leaving a larger pool for reenlistment.

Figure 4.4
First-Term Reenlistment Rate for Personnel with a Four-Year Term of Service, by Service and IT Group, FYs 1997–2001

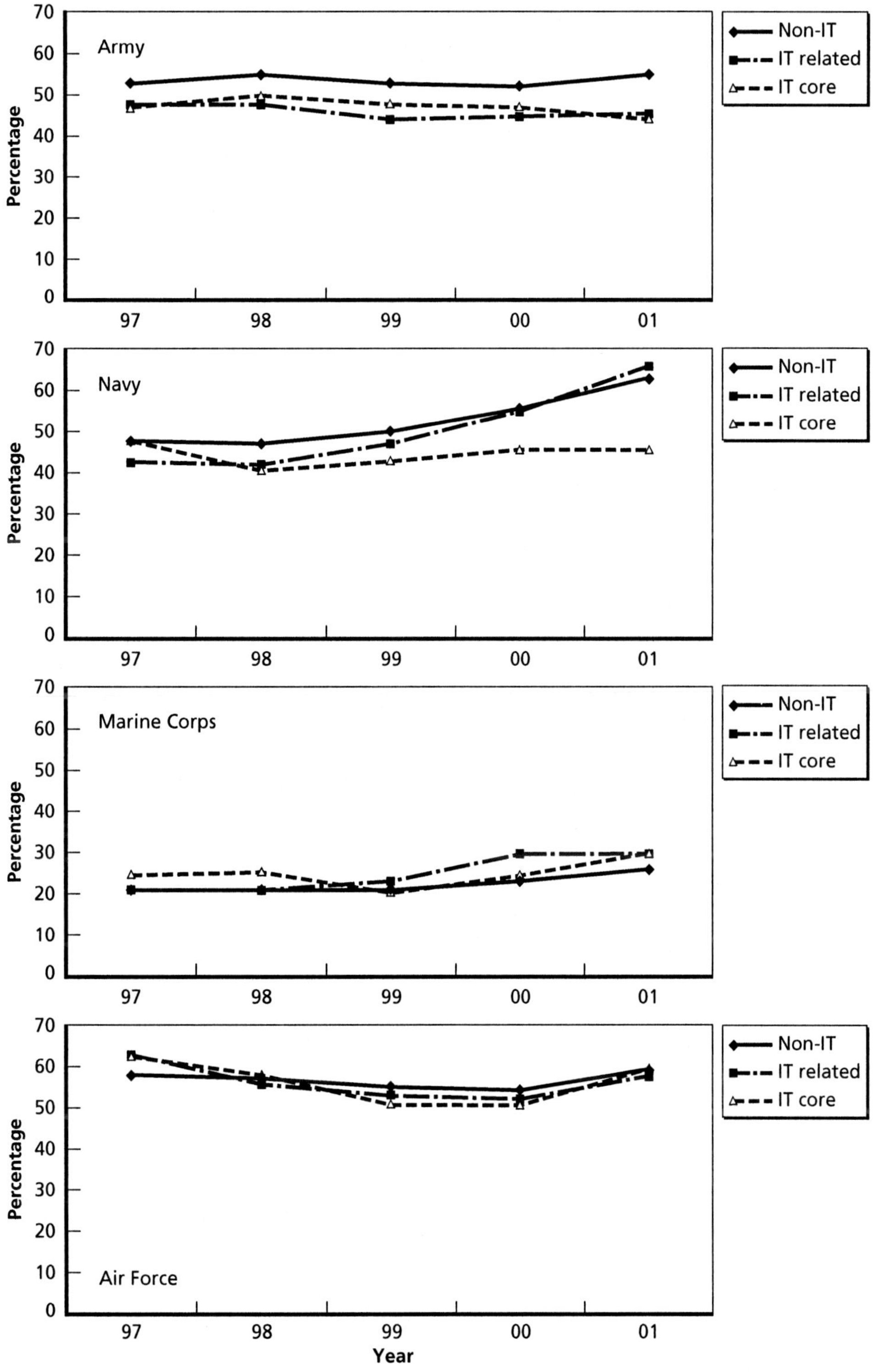

RAND *MG108-4.4*

ditional training is another factor. If personnel expect to obtain further valuable training in IT by remaining in service, this should increase IT reenlistment. Thus, the various factors do not point to a clear implication that IT reenlistment should be lower than non-IT reenlistment.

The predicted probabilities of reenlistment by AFQT are shown in Table 4.7. In the Army, reenlistment is lower in IT than in non-IT, and reenlistment declines as AFQT rises. Navy reenlistment is also lower in IT than in non-IT, but reenlistment rises with AFQT. Perhaps the Navy offers additional valuable training in IT and it is more attractive to high-AFQT sailors. Marine Corps reenlistment is higher in IT than in non-IT for members with an AFQT score of 50 or higher (i.e., categories IIIA, II, and I), but about the same for lower scores (category IIIB). Low-AFQT Marines might not be competitive for the relatively small number of reenlistment slots. Air Force reenlistment is higher in IT than non-IT, but reenlistment declines with AFQT. In the top AFQT category, there is no difference in reenlistment between IT and non-IT. Career development opportunities may be high in non-IT as well as IT positions in the Air Force, i.e., IT does not have an edge.

Table 4.7
Predicted Probability of First-Term Reenlistment in IT and Non-IT Occupations, by AFQT Category

	Army		Navy		Marine Corps		Air Force	
Variable	Non-IT	IT	Non-IT	IT	Non-IT	IT	Non-IT	IT
AFQT I–II	.46	.43	.65	.63	.24	.26	.55	.55
AFQT IIIA	.49	.46	.56	.53	.23	.26	.56	.60
AFQT IIIB	.50	.46	.54	.50	.22	.23	.59	.65

Observations

The preceding discussion used data and regression analysis to show that IT occupations are able to attract high-quality recruits, to induce some of them to select longer terms, to maintain lower attrition rates, and to achieve comparable reenlistment rates to non-IT occupations. It is not uncommon for the percentage of high-quality recruits to be 10 to 20 points higher in IT than non-IT, and AFQT scores in IT occupations average 10 to 20 points higher or more, a very large difference. Initial terms of service are more than twice as likely to be long, five or six years, in IT than in non-IT in the Marine Corps and the Army. Furthermore, the loss of first-term personnel through attrition is over a third lower in IT than in non-IT in the Air Force, Navy, and Marine Corps, and slightly lower in the Army. Reenlistment is lower in IT than in non-IT in the Army and the Navy, slightly higher in the Marine Corps, and about the same in the Air Force. Finally, our findings support the hypothesis that IT training is more valuable to high-AFQT personnel.

These observations and the results of our analysis run counter to what one might have expected during the period of peak private-sector demand for IT workers. The popular press carried reports of a surging demand for IT workers and a spiraling competition among employers obliged to offer high pay, access to the latest information technology, time for training, and support for career development. Yet the military excelled in attracting and keeping high-quality recruits in IT. When there were difficulties in recruiting in FY 1998, IT recruiting did not fare any worse than other recruiting. Over and above the importance of such factors as recruiting resources, recruiter effort, enlistment incentives, and advertising, it seems that the value and transferability of IT training provided a key advantage in the military's success.

CHAPTER FIVE

Wages in Information Technology

This chapter looks at the relative difference between civilian and military wages in IT and non-IT occupations. We find that private-sector wages in IT for persons with a high school diploma or some college are well above wages in non-IT occupations. However, military pay does not differ much by service or specialty, and as a result, higher private-sector wages in IT mean that military pay is relatively low for IT occupations generally.[1] Our findings are apparently contradictory: relatively lower military pay in IT versus success in recruiting and retaining high-quality personnel in IT. This dilemma can be resolved, as we have suggested, by recognizing the value to the individual of the IT skills and training offered by the military. An IT recruit can leave the military with certified IT skills, qualify for IT jobs in the private sector, and have the military pick up the tab for training. In effect, military IT training and experience are a compensating differential for the relatively low military pay in IT.[2]

However, although the opportunity to receive training may increase a recruit's willingness to receive a lower salary in a military IT position, an enlisted member, having specialized in IT, has an incentive to leave the military for a higher paying civilian IT job. An individual's decision to stay in the military will depend on whether the military can offer a comparable career opportunity to that in the civilian sector. The provision of additional training and education, the chance for further professional growth, the satisfaction from performing military duties, the support for spouse and family, and the level of military relative to civilian pay may all bear on the choice to reenlist.

To gain a better understanding of these issues and the impact that wage levels have on recruitment and retention rates, this chapter considers two questions:

- Have civilian wages been higher and grown faster in IT occupations than in non-IT occupations?
- How well did military pay compare with civilian wages in IT and non-IT occupations?

[1] Bonuses and educational benefits add to regular military compensation and can be used to offset higher civilian pay. Our limited evidence suggests little difference in enlistment bonus usage across our three occupational groups (see Table 5.3). Also, military pay by years of service is similar across one-digit occupational groups (Asch, Hosek, and Martin, 2002), where the computation of military pay includes regular military compensation, special and incentive pays, and miscellaneous allowances and cost of living adjustments and accounts for possible differences in promotion speed.

[2] It is also possible that military IT jobs have better work conditions and amenities than non-IT jobs, quite apart from post-service earnings potential. Lack of data prevents a comparison of work conditions and amenities for IT and non-IT military positions.

We approach these questions with a regression analysis of civilian wages from 1983 to 2002 and with nonparametric wage percentile tabulations based on 1997–2002 civilian wage data. The regression analysis identifies factors affecting the wages of non-IT, IT-related, and IT–core occupations over a two-decade period for men and women. It also affords a basis for discussing the results in the context of research on the monetary benefits from education. The nonparametric wage percentiles reflect the actual data,[3] and we use the nonparametric results in the next chapter. Our measure of military compensation is regular military compensation, as discussed below. We also briefly comment on bonus usage in military IT and non-IT occupations.

Methodology

Defining Our Sample

To parallel Chapter Four, in our analysis of civilian wages we define three groups to classify occupations in the economy: IT core, IT related, and non-IT. Table 5.1 lists the IT-core and IT-related occupations. The IT-core occupations are civilian counterparts to the IT occupations identified in the Department of Defense study of information technology/information assurance personnel (U.S. Office of the Secretary of Defense, 1999, Appendix E) and include programmers, system administrators, database managers, technicians, operators, analysts, and IT creators.

The mix of IT-core occupations tends to vary with education level. At the level of high school and some college, IT-core occupations are likely to be technical and operational, and at the level of four or more years of college, they are likely to include scientists, engineers, analysts, and IT creators. We chose IT-related occupations with the intent of selecting occupations that directly and heavily relied on computing. We also included telecommunications worker, as we did for the military. IT-related occupations are largely professional but include such not-so-clearly "professional" occupations as communications equipment operator, electrician, and electrical power equipment operator.

Defining Our Data

For civilian wages, our data on weekly wages came from the monthly outgoing rotation of the Current Population Survey (CPS) from January 1983 through March 2002, a period of nearly 20 years. We limited the sample to full-time workers (35 or more hours of work per week) age 17 to 55.[4] Weekly wages reflect compensation during a typical week and include

[3] We considered fitting percentile regressions to data for 1997–2002, but some exploration with these regressions suggested they would add little beyond the nonparametric computations. Percentile regressions would in effect smooth aberrations in the nonparametric percentiles, but the latter appeared smooth to begin with. In other exploratory work, we computed wage percentiles from the regressions for 1983–2002, but we abandoned this approach because of the possibility of specification error (or imprecise fit) for recent years, while the nonparametric analysis for 1997–2002 data has no such problem.

[4] The most relevant age range for the military is shorter, say, 17–35. We included ages 17–55 to estimate the curvature of the age-experience profile accurately. Including the older workers does not bias our comparisons; even though more experienced workers generally have higher wages, our regressions and our graphics control for experience.

Table 5.1
IT-Core and IT-Related Occupations in the Economy

IT Core
Computer systems analyst and scientist
Operations and systems researcher and analyst
Computer science teacher
Electrical and electronic technician
Broadcast equipment operator
Computer programmer
Tool programmer, numerical control
Supervisor, computer equipment operators
Supervisor, financial records processing
Computer operator
Peripheral equipment operator
IT Related
Financial manager
Architect
Engineer and engineering technician
Surveyor and mapping scientist
Actuary, bookkeeper, auditor
Scientist (math, physics, space, etc.)
Air traffic controller
Communications equipment operator
Supervisor
Billing, posting, calculating machine operator
Electrician and electrical power equipment operator
Numerical control machine operator

usual overtime if any.[5] They do not include employer-paid contributions to health insurance, retirement, or other benefits, or year-end bonuses or stock options.

The civilian weekly wages are comparable to "regular military compensation" (the sum of basic pay, basic allowance for subsistence, basic allowance for housing, and a federal tax advantage due to the nontaxability of the allowances). RMC accounts for over 90 percent of a service member's cash pay on average (Asch, Hosek, and Martin, 2002). The remainder of cash income comes from special and incentive pays, e.g., bonuses, hazardous duty pay, and sea pay, plus miscellaneous allowances and cost-of-living adjustments. RMC does not include retirement benefits or health benefits. To a good approximation, the weekly wage and regular military compensation both represent current cash pay, i.e., take-home pay.

We deflated wages and military pay to FY 2002 dollars by the Urban Consumer Price Index (CPI) minus 0.5 percent. For instance, if the price index rose by 3.5 percent, we used a deflator of 3.0 percent. This adjustment is consistent with recent research on the CPI

[5] The questions in the CPS are as follows. For 1979–1993, we used questions 25A, 25C, and 25D: "How many hours per week does . . . USUALLY work at this job?" "How much does . . . earn per hour?" and "How much does . . . USUALLY earn per week at this job BEFORE deductions? Include any overtime pay, commissions, or tips usually received." For 1994 and later, we used the variable for weekly earnings, "ERNWK," which includes overtime pay, tips, and commissions. The questions were "What are (name's/your) usual weekly earnings on (this job/(your/his/her) MAIN job) before taxes or other deductions?"

at the Bureau of Labor Statistics and reduces the upward bias in the CPI caused by substitution bias, outlet bias, and quality bias.[6]

The basic wage specification used in our analysis was

$$\textit{ln}\text{ weekly wage}_t = \beta_0 + \beta_1\text{Hispanic} + \beta_2\text{Black} + \beta_3\text{Experience} + \beta_4\text{Experience-squared} + \beta_5\text{Unemployment rate} + \beta_6\text{Time} + \varepsilon_t.$$

However, the coefficients are allowed to differ by education level and by occupation group. We estimated separate models for men and women. Four education levels (less than high school, high school, some college, and four or more years of college) and three occupation groups (IT core, IT related, and other) produced 12 sets of coefficients for each gender. The experience variable is defined as age minus years of school completed minus six.[7] Time is measured in months beginning with January 1983. The unemployment rate is the national unemployment rate as of the month of the wage observation. We assume that the random error in the log wage specification is normally distributed with zero mean and constant variance, and we estimate the model by ordinary least squares (OLS) on unweighted data.[8]

There are certain limitations to this analysis given the difficulty of controlling for individual ability and other factors and the difficulty of precisely recording an individual's education level. The wage equation is a reduced form. It quantifies the wage structure of IT and non-IT occupations but does not identify the underlying labor demand and supply behaviors that interact to produce the structure. In particular, the wage analysis does not estimate the economic return to additional schooling. As the literature emphasizes, in a regression of the wage on the level of schooling the schooling coefficient may be biased by the omission of variables for ability, motivation, family inputs, and financial aid. Furthermore, the reported level of education may contain errors. Omitted variables, such as ability, bias the education coefficient upward, while measurement errors in education bias the coefficient downward.

In one vein of work, researchers have used standardized test scores and family background variables to control for omitted variables, while in another they have studied twins with different years of schooling.[9] Although the CPS contains data on family income and the

---

[6] When the price of a good rises, consumers buy less of that good and more of substitute goods whose prices have not risen. Discount outlets often sell products at lower prices than ordinary retail outlets, and the spread of discount outlets has in effect lowered prices. The quality of many products improves over time through technological advances, but it is difficult to account for in the construction of price indexes. For a more detailed discussion, see articles in the symposium "Measuring the CPI," *Journal of Economic Perspectives*, Vol. 12, No. 1, Winter 1998, pp. 3–78. Our 0.5 percent adjustment to the CPI is in keeping with the adjustment suggested by the Bureau of Labor Statistics in its research on CPI bias (Stewart and Reed, 1999).

[7] In a small number of cases, this approximation produced a negative number for the initial level of experience, as when a person graduated from college at a very young age. In such cases, we set experience to zero.

[8] Estimates produced from weighted data were virtually identical to estimates produced using unweighted data.

[9] The literature on returns to schooling is voluminous, but a brief, accessible discussion is contained in Bonjour et al., 2002. Their Table 2, p. 14, summarizes estimates of the return to education from a number of different studies. Hogan and Rigoban (2002) developed a new estimator based on the heteroscedasticity of individual wages and education levels, which allowed them to control for unobserved ability, measurement error, and the endogeneity of education. Lillard and Kilburn (unpublished) argue that within a family, standardized test scores are codetermined with the level of school; test scores at a given grade are observed only for students who have chosen to continue in school, and the decision to continue depends on previous and anticipated test scores. Their argument calls into question the customary approach of including test score as a control for ability in a wage regression, especially when studying the wages of young workers. They specify a model with equations for continuing in school, test score, labor force participation, and wage given participation. Other research has focused on an individual's comparative advantage as a determinant of education level and occupational choice. This

number and ages of siblings, it does not include data on standardized test scores, the availability of financial aid, or identifiers for twins. The education coefficients in Table 5.2 reflect the combined effect of the return to education, ability effects associated with education, and errors in the reported level of education.[10,11]

In addition, our wage analysis is limited because it takes the level of education as given when, in reality, individuals choose their level of education. A child's educational attainment depends on family income, parents' education, number of siblings, and other factors such as whether the family recently immigrated. Further, whether a person attends college depends on verbal and quantitative aptitude, tuition and fees, and financial aid.

In thinking about the wage comparisons, it is useful not only to view them from the perspective of workers who have completed their education, but also from the perspective of individuals who are deciding whether to obtain more education and are considering the expected benefits from it. The military wants high-aptitude recruits; yet high-aptitude individuals are likely to opt for college.[12] A high school graduate may be thinking of attending a community college or a four-year college or university, and to attract this individual the military must offer a package competitive with those paths. In addition to satisfaction derived from military service, the package may include skill training, bonuses, and educational benefits.

Regression Analysis of Civilian Wages

Table 5.2 contains the regression results. The entries in the table with a superscripted note indicate coefficients that are *not* statistically significant at a level of 0.05. Most coefficients are significant and in most cases have high levels of significance ($p < 0.0001$) because of the large sample size (about 1.4 million observations for each gender). In many cases, the IT-related and the IT-core coefficients differ by much more than two standard errors of the coefficients from the non-IT coefficients, pointing to a statistically significant difference.

The regressions for men show by inspection little difference in the wage structures for IT-core and non-IT occupations at the high school level. In particular, the intercepts and

approach, which can be seen as an outgrowth of the need to control for "ability," views career choice as the solution of a dynamic programming problem that also involves education and training choice. For example, see Keane and Wolpin (1997).

10 Changes in the CPS question format also affect the reported level of education. Before 1992, CPS education questions were oriented around the highest grade completed. They then changed to report the highest degree received. In 1997, questions were added to allow comparison between reported levels of education in the pre- and post-1992 formats. Jaeger (2002) found that the highest grade completed was a tenth of a year higher in the post-1992 format. This has the effect of making the estimated return to education lower; Jaeger estimates that the return is lower by 0.6 to 1.0 percentage points.

11 Nevertheless, the education coefficients may be "near" the true return to education. Bonjour et al. (2002) found, among other things, that the ability bias and reporting error bias offset each other; so their corrected estimate of the return to schooling was close to their "uncorrected" OLS estimate. Hogan and Rigoban's (2002) preferred estimate is also close to their OLS estimate. They interpret this as indicating that the biases due to unobserved ability and to measurement error offset each other.

12 As one indication of this relationship, consider the average AFQT score given educational attainment at age 30 for white males who had graduated from high school by age 20. For those with no further education beyond high school, average AFQT was 50. For those with some college, it was 65, and for those with four or more years of college, it was 84. The data are from the National Longitudinal Study of Youth; AFQT scores are from 1980; and the estimations are based on authors' tabulations.

Table 5.2
Regression Results for ln Weekly Wage–Civilian Workers (standard error)

	Men			Women		
	Non-IT	IT Related	IT Core	Non-IT	IT Related	IT Core
Less than high school						
Intercept	5.10124	5.56189	4.86242	4.70271	4.97842	4.99623
	(.01299)	(.09310)	(.23961)	(.01725)	(.12516)	(.24331)
Black	–.19550	–.16554	–.16165	.01496	.04756[a]	.00489
	(.00455)	(.03952)	(.08692)	(.00544)	(.05445)	(.08387)
Hispanic	–.02474	–.07381	.06526[a]	.06399	.13158	.01928[a]
	(.00429)	(.03418)	(.08713)	(.00635)	(.04808)	(.09865)
Experience	.10850	.08149	.13820	.08154	.08655	.10788
	(.00040)	(.00317)	(.00682)	(.00052)	(.00403)	(.00781)
Experience squared	–.00207	–.00142	–.00272	–.00160	–.00176	–.00220
	(.00001)	(.00008)	(.00020)	(.00001)	(.00011)	(.00022)
Unemployment rate	–.01500	–.01362[a]	.00860[a]	–.00795	.00040	–.00146[a]
	(.00159)	(.01117)	(.02936)	(.00212)	(.01501)	(.03040)
Time	–.00072	–.00077	.00014[a]	.00006[a]	–.00031[a]	–.00065[a]
	(.00003)	(.00024)	(.00060)	(.00004)	(.00033)	(.00069)
High school						
Intercept	5.69160	5.97901	5.66381	5.32641	5.67737	5.55115
	(.00724)	(.02954)	(.06155)	(.00846)	(.03168)	(.05930)
Black	–.23598	–.14899	–.17340	.02058	.13438	.01059[a]
	(.00267)	(.01380)	(.02486)	(.00288)	(.01402)	(.02222)
Hispanic	–.13332	–.10407	–.09425	.00506	.06920	.00330[a]
	(.00316)	(.01571)	(.03093)	(.00399)	(.01678)	(.03093)
Experience	.07169	.05712	.07862	.04367	.03281	.04771
	(.00029)	(.00131)	(.00265)	(.00033)	(.00144)	(.00265)
Experience squared	–.00137	–.00101	–.00148	–.00086	–.00065	–.00096
	(.00001)	(.00003)	(.00007)	(.00001)	(.00004)	(.00007)
Unemployment rate	–.01304	–.00765	.00768[a]	–.00655	–.00849	.01001[a]
	(.00087)	(.00345)	(.00734)	(.00102)	(.00368)	(.00714)
Time	–.00046	–.00030	.00020[a]	.00031	.00044	.00058
	(.00002)	(.00007)	(.00015)	(.00002)	(.00008)	(.00016)
Some college						
Intercept	5.56269	6.01692	5.78090	5.30196	5.64461	5.65422
	(.00956)	(.02766)	(.04316)	(.01043)	(.03479)	(.06149)
Black	–.17369	–.11612	–.11093	.05272	.11855	–.04479
	(.00353)	(.01184)	(.01769)	(.00340)	(.01245)	(.02018)
Hispanic	–.07297	–.07642	–.04450	.03592	.08734	–.01918[a]
	(.00427)	(.01346)	(.02110)	(.00491)	(.01671)	(.03431)
Experience	.10680	.07528	.09586	.07555	.05063	.08253
	(.00034)	(.00112)	(.00167)	(.00036)	(.00138)	(.00251)
Experience squared	–.00229	–.00150	–.00203	–.00167	–.00110	–.00188
	(.00001)	(.00003)	(.00005)	(.00001)	(.00004)	(.00008)
Unemployment rate	–.01874	–.01961	–.01117	–.01078	–.00997	–.01476
	(.00115)	(.00332)	(.00527)	(.00127)	(.00419)	(.00761)
Time	–.00030	–.00029	.00008[a]	.00014	.00045	.00035
	(.00002)	(.00007)	(.00011)	(.00003)	(.00009)	(.00015)
4+ years of college						
Intercept	6.07656	6.48692	6.43296	5.93301	6.17898	6.23802
	(.00998)	(.01996)	(.03634)	(.01130)	(.03629)	(.05872)
Black	–.21566	–.18464	–.12860	.05717	–.01469	–.11245
	(.00473)	(.01133)	(.01759)	(.00440)	(.01458)	(.02187)

Table 5.2—continued

	Men			Women		
	Non-IT	IT Related	IT Core	Non-IT	IT Related	IT Core
Hispanic	−.16270	−.08101	−.09031	−.03189	−.00547	−.04768[a]
	(.00598)	(.01306)	(.02429)	(.00678)	(.02178)	(.03848)
Experience	.07614	.05068	.05181	.03972	.02296	.03654
	(.00046)	(.00092)	(.00165)	(.00049)	(.00159)	(.00267)
Experience squared	−.00167	−.00107	−.00116	−.00093	−.00072	−.00093
	(.00001)	(.00003)	(.00005)	(.00002)	(.00005)	(.00009)
Unemployment rate	−.01206	−.00952	−.01416	−.00833	−.00163[a]	−.00244[a]
	(.00118)	(.00239)	(.00441)	(.00136)	(.00446)	(.00728)
Time	.00047	.00030	.00079	.00102	.00142	.00129
	(.00002)	(.00005)	(.00009)	(.00003)	(.00009)	(.00015)
R-squared	.99			.99		
MSE	.55984			.64624		
Observations	1,442,114			1,378,853		

NOTES: Most coefficients are significant and have high levels of significance ($p < 0.001$) because of the large sample size. MSE is mean squared error.

[a]These coefficients are *not* statistically significant at a level of 0.05.

experience coefficients are about the same for the two groups. The similarity between IT-core and non-IT occupations suggests that IT-core workers at the high school level have skill sets that are no more highly valued than those of non-IT workers, who are the majority of workers. By comparison, the intercept for IT-related occupations is higher, and, in a pattern seen throughout the table, the higher intercept is accompanied by a lower coefficient on experience. That is, the wage starts at a higher level and grows more slowly with experience.

The similarity between IT-core and non-IT occupations disappears at higher levels of education. Instead, IT-related and IT-core occupations are comparatively close to one another and distant from non-IT. For men with some college, wages in IT-core occupations are higher than in non-IT occupations, as seen by the higher intercept, though the highest wages are in IT-related occupations.[13] For men with four or more years of college, the wages in IT-core and IT-related occupations are practically the same. Presumably both occupational groups consist of professions, and both are well above the non-IT wage structure.

The results also indicate a difference in wage trends, shown by the coefficient on the time variable. For those with high school and some college education, the wage trend is negative for non-IT and IT-related occupations but essentially zero for IT-core occupations. A coefficient of −0.0003 seems small, but cumulated over the 240 months from January 1983 to January 2003, it accounts for a 7.2 percent decline in real wages ($-0.0003 \times 240 = 0.072$). That is, wages in non-IT and IT-related occupations fell by about 7 percent, while wages in IT-core occupations held constant or grew slightly.[14] In contrast, wages for college graduates trended up, and the trend was largest for IT-core occupations. The predicted overall increase from January 1983 to January 2003 is 11 percent in non-IT occupations, 7 percent in IT-

[13] In the nonparametric results below for recent years, wages are nearly equal in IT core and IT related.

[14] The time coefficient for IT core is not statistically different from zero for men with high school or some college education.

related occupations, and 19 percent in IT-core occupations. These differences are statistically significant.

For women with high school education, initial wages are highest in IT related, followed by IT core, and then by non-IT. Wages grow with experience fastest in IT core, however. With some college education, wages for women with little experience are about the same in IT related and IT core yet again grow fastest in IT core. With four or more years of college education, wages are highest in IT core and grow at about the same rate as in non-IT. For women with high school education or more, all time effects are positive and exceed the respective effects for men. Over this period, therefore, women's wages increased relative to men's. Time effects for women are especially large at the college level. The percentage increases in wages, calculated as above, are huge: 24 percent for non-IT, 34 percent for IT related, and 31 percent for IT core.

Military/Civilian Wage Comparisons

As we suggested at the start of this chapter, we are interested in looking at the differences between civilian and military wages in the IT and non-IT sectors to better understand the compensation choice facing potential recruits. To compare RMC with civilian wages, we computed civilian wage percentiles from data for 1997–2002 and then smoothed them, and we computed the expected level of RMC over a 20-year military career from military pay tables and recent speeds of promotion. Civilian wages are in FY 2002 dollars, and military pay is based on January 2002 pay tables. We computed promotion speeds with data from the Defense Manpower Data Center.

Construction of Civilian Wage Percentiles and RMC

The civilian wage percentiles are based on data from January 1997 through March 2002. To obtain percentile curves, we proceeded nonparametrically, first computing the wage at the 10th through 90th percentiles for data grouped by IT occupation group, education level, gender, and experience. The experience groups were three years wide and spanned a total of 30 years of experience. Within each occupation group, gender, and education level, we smoothed the percentile curves by fitting fourth-degree polynomials to wages by experience. This produced the wage percentiles in Figures 5.1–5.4 for men with some college, men with four or more years of college, women with some college, and women with four or more years of college.

As a reminder, RMC is the sum of basic pay, basic allowance for housing,[15] basic allowance for subsistence, and the tax advantage deriving from the nontaxability of the allowances. We computed RMC pay lines by service for enlisted personnel and for officers, but not by occupational group and gender.[16] Therefore, the RMC lines by service are the same across the panels in each figure for non-IT, IT related, and IT core, and the RMC lines for

---

[15] Enlisted members live in barracks during basic and advanced training, and the value of this housing is presumably lower than the value implied by RMC. As a result, RMC might overstate military pay during this time.

[16] We did not have promotion speed data by gender or by occupation. The RMC lines should therefore be viewed as an approximation for any given group.

enlisted men are the same as those for enlisted women, and similarly for officers. We have limited the range of experience in Figures 5.1–5.4 to 20 years.[17]

We focus on the "some college" level of education for enlisted members for several reasons. The services need to recruit from the college market if they are to meet their goals for high-quality recruits. Today, two-thirds of high school graduates obtain some college, compared with 50 percent 20 years ago. In addition, many members who enter service with a high school education add to that education while in service. The percentage of personnel who report their level of education as some college has risen substantially since the 1980s, and members are increasingly likely to begin using their GI Bill educational benefit while in service.[18] This means that the civilian opportunity wage of the modal enlisted member is well represented by the some-college civilian wage.

Note on Bonuses

It is important for our analysis to note that although the services use bonuses as enlistment and reenlistment incentives, RMC omits bonuses. Bonuses provide DoD with a way to respond fairly quickly to anticipated shortfalls in retention, and research has shown that bonuses are an effective incentive even though uncertainty remains over the size of their effect on retention (e.g., Goldberg, 2002). Although bonuses are effective, their use is limited, as seen in Table 5.3. The table is based on tabulations from FY 1999 Joint Uniformed Military Pay System (JUMPS) data. The table shows the percentage of members receiving a bonus and the average amount of the bonus received.

As noted previously, there was no clear pattern across the services of higher incidence or higher amounts of enlistment bonuses in IT occupations than in non-IT occupations. In the Army, about 20 percent of first-year personnel received an enlistment bonus, and this

Table 5.3
Enlistment and Reenlistment Bonus Incidence and Average Amount, FY 1999

	Percentage Receiving			Average Amount		
Type of Bonus	Non-IT	IT Related	IT Core	Non-IT	IT Related	IT Core
Enlistment bonus						
Army	21	20	21	$6,449	$6,311	$2,966
Navy	13	24	23	$2,459	$3,326	$5,269
Marine Corps	5	3	4	$2,464	$2,000	$1,667
Air Force	54	39	23	$3,743	$3,589	$2,701
Reenlistment bonus						
Army	18	21	20	$5,475	$6,854	$5,215
Navy	10	14	15	$20,463	$24,347	$26,037
Marine Corps	4	8	10	$8,715	$15,828	$15,841
Air Force	23	18	17	$10,722	$11,167	$13,285

NOTE: Values were computed for members present in all 12 months of FY 1999. Enlistment and reenlistment bonus values are based on the "original entitlement," which represents the full size of the bonus rather than the initial payment. Reenlistment bonus values are for members reenlisting in the fourth year of service.

[17] Over the 20–30 year range, our RMC rises rapidly relative to civilian wages. This is an artifact of the exit of lower-ranking personnel when they reach retirement eligibility. The highest levels of the military pay scale are reached by a small percentage of personnel, and RMC at the highest ranks typically exceeds the 90th percentile of civilian wages.

[18] See Asch, Hosek, and Warner (2001) for further discussion of these points.

percentage was about the same across occupational groups. In the Navy, over 20 percent of IT personnel received a bonus, compared with 13 percent of non-IT personnel. The Marine Corps made the least use of bonuses, with only 3 to 5 percent of first-term members receiving a bonus. In the Air Force, 54 percent of non-IT members received a bonus, which compares with 39 percent of IT-related and 23 percent of IT-core members. In most cases, the average bonus was less than $4,000, or about $1,000/year for a four-year enlistment. However, IT bonuses averaged over $5,000 in Navy IT-core occupations, and in the Army the bonuses of non-IT and IT-related were over $6,000, while the bonus for IT was about $3,000.

Regarding reenlistment bonuses, overall, first-term reenlistment bonus usage and amounts tended to be higher in IT-core and IT-related than in non-IT occupations, and the reenlistment bonuses were considerably higher than the enlistment bonuses. The reenlistment bonuses were allocated evenly across occupations groups in the Army, as was the case with Army enlistment bonuses. In the Navy, bonus usage was higher in IT than non-IT; 10 percent of members in non-IT occupations received a bonus, compared with about 15 percent in IT occupations. The Marine Corps again made the least use of bonuses; yet bonus usage was higher in IT than non-IT (8–10 percent versus 4 percent). In the Air Force, 23 percent of non-IT members received a bonus, while 17–18 percent of IT members received a bonus. In most cases, reenlistment bonuses averaged several thousand dollars more in IT than non-IT occupations. The exception was the Army, where bonuses were only $5,000–$6,000 or so regardless of occupation. But in the Navy, non-IT bonuses were about $20,000, while IT bonuses were about $25,000, and the respective figures for the Marine Corps were roughly $9,000 and $16,000. Air Force bonuses were about $11,000 for non-IT and IT related and $13,000 for IT core.

The Army, Navy, and Air Force sought large increases in their bonus budgets in the late 1990s in the face of enlistment and retention difficulties. For instance, the Army enlistment bonus budget rose from about $100 million to $130 million from FY 1999 to FY 2002. The comparable increase for the Navy was $50 million to $105 million, and for the Air Force $25 million to $130 million (Asch et al., 2002, pp. 54–55). As a result, bonus usage, and perhaps bonus amounts, increased in recent years.

Promotion Speed

Because promotions in military rank affect the wages earned by an individual service member, a closer look at the prevalence and speed of promotion is useful in our wage comparison. Table 5.4 presents the mean and variance of promotion speeds by pay grade for FYs 1981–1999.

Changes in promotion speed over these years were minor, as evidenced by the relatively small standard deviation of time in grade to promotion. In most cases, the standard deviation was around 10 percent of the average number of months in grade at time of promotion. An exception to this is E-5 in the Air Force, where average months in grade at time to promotion increased from 30–35 months in the early 1980s to about 55 months in the

Table 5.4
Average (μ) and Standard Deviation (σ) of Months in Grade at Time of Promotion, 1981–1999

	Army		Navy		Marine Corps		Air Force	
Group	μ	σ	μ	σ	μ	σ	μ	σ
Enlisted								
E-2	7.73	0.88	8.63	1.07	6.96	0.25	6.64	0.72
E-3	10.16	0.19	11.57	0.55	10.03	0.41	10.40	0.79
E-4	13.67	1.49	17.26	1.42	20.13	2.85	22.16	1.69
E-5	31.15	4.05	31.85	6.57	27.19	6.40	45.41	10.83
E-6	49.54	4.85	57.75	12.05	55.67	7.35	78.37	8.61
E-7	68.78	7.43	74.56	5.29	67.44	7.86	58.39	5.10
E-8	74.48	6.52	70.04	5.19	73.25	7.35	61.88	8.87
E-9	62.10	4.06	58.67	3.68	61.47	3.83	51.28	6.58
Officers								
O-2	22.22	3.24	24.35	1.29	24.03	0.39	24.11	0.34
O-3	27.64	3.54	25.51	0.64	33.07	3.75	24.22	0.11
O-4	86.11	5.42	67.69	5.81	73.35	7.66	90.08	5.20
O-5	68.67	6.33	69.39	3.59	70.29	6.72	61.76	3.17
O-6	70.52	5.38	74.94	3.05	66.65	5.03	65.33	4.46
O-7	65.36	8.82	80.94	5.12	59.88	7.34	79.72	5.81
O-8	42.34	5.24	35.61	4.94	38.19	7.52	38.59	4.50
O-9	54.07	27.62	38.11	20.37	49.70	30.58	54.35	22.68
O-10	28.91	10.12	31.76	17.20	18.37	15.22	36.29	7.89

SOURCE: Authors' tabulations from data provided by the Defense Manpower Data Center.

1990s after the defense manpower draw down. We used the average promotion speeds for FYs 1997–1999, the most recent years available, to compute RMC by years of service.[19]

Wage Comparisons for Men

Our wage comparisons for men (Figures 5.1 and 5.2) show that civilian wages for men are higher in IT than non-IT and therefore that military pay is relatively lower in IT than non-IT. The data in Figures 5.1 and 5.2 show civilian wage percentiles by IT occupational group for men with some college (meaning a year or two of college but not four years) and for men with four or more years of college. The upper panel is for non-IT occupations, the center panel for IT-related occupations, and the lower panel for IT-core occupations. RMC pay lines by service overlay these percentiles. Also, because many officers obtain a graduate degree, we also made comparisons for men and women with more than four years of college. These are shown in Appendix C.

For men with some college, RMC begins at the 90th percentile of wages in non-IT occupations (upper panel in Figure 5.1), moves to the 70th percentile for years of experience 7 through 16, then rises to between the 70th and 80th percentile for years 17 through 20. For IT-related occupations, RMC begins at the 70th percentile and lies between the 50th and 60th for most years of experience. For IT-core occupations, RMC starts at the 70th percentile, declines to between the 40th and 50th percentile, and rises to between the 50th and 60th percentile near 20 years of experience. As experience increases, the movement of RMC

[19] We also computed RMC pay lines with the average promotion speeds over the entire period, 1981–1999, and found very little difference in the results.

to higher percentiles derives from the promotion of enlisted members to the noncommissioned officer (NCO) ranks of E-5, E-6, and E-7.

We interpret a starting value of RMC at the 90th percentile with caution. For men and women with some college (Figures 5.1 and 5.3), we were surprised by the large percentage of civilian wages less than $200 per week in the first few years of experience. Although the wage computations are limited to workers who worked full time (35 or more hours) in the survey week, workers may have been trying out different occupations and employers and may have been motivated more by a desire to experience different jobs, employers, and occupations than by wage. Also, despite working full time in the survey week, some workers who planned to go to college might have taken a readily available job. Employers, for their part, might have been willing to offer a position to an inexperienced worker to see whether he or she would "work out."

For men with four or more years of college (Figure 5.2), RMC hovers around the 80th percentile of wages in non-IT occupations over the entire range of experience shown. For IT-related occupations, RMC starts at the 50th percentile, moves up to between the 70th and 80th percentile for 5–12 years of experience, stays at the 80th until the 17th year, then increases to between the 80th and 90th. For IT-core occupations, RMC starts between the 40th and 50th percentile and rises to the 60th–70th percentile, where it lies for 5–12 years of experience. RMC is at the 70th-80th percentile for 13–17 years of experience and the 80th-90th percentile for 18–20 years of experience. The increases in RMC relative to civilian wages reflect the increase in military pay that comes with promotion to the ranks of O-3, O-4, and O-5 (e.g., captain, major, and lieutenant colonel, or, in the Navy, lieutenant, lieutenant commander, and commander).

Wage Comparisons for Women

When interpreting the pay comparisons for women, it is useful to recall that these are essentially cross-sectional pay comparisons, not life-cycle comparisons. Wage data from 1997–2002 are stated in year 2002 dollars and treated as a single large cross section. Yet as the regression analysis found, the time trend in women's wages has been larger than that of men, that is, women's wages have risen relative to men's. The wages of women with high school, some college, or four or more years of college have risen at rates comparable to the wage increases for men with four or more years of college. This increase suggests that the life-cycle wages of recent labor-force entry cohorts of women will lie above those of older cohorts. As a result, the cross-sectional wage profiles by years of experience are probably flatter than the life-cycle profiles. Women entering the labor force today can therefore expect higher lifetime earnings than the cross-sectional comparisons shown in Figures 5.3 and 5.4 suggest. With respect to military/civilian pay, if RMC were at the 80th wage percentile at 15 years of experience in the cross-section, it would be less than the 80th percentile in a life-cycle comparison. Stated more generally, the RMC-civilian wage comparisons in Figures 5.3 and 5.4 probably *overstate* military pay relative to civilian pay because younger cohorts of women can expect higher civilian pay as they gain experience than the pay shown in the cross section. This is not as much of a concern for men (Figures 5.1 and 5.2) because their civilian wage trends have been small, except for men with four or more years of college, and as a result the cross-sectional wage profiles are probably close to life-cycle profiles.

Figure 5.1
Weekly Civilian Wage Percentiles for Men with Some College and Regular Military Compensation for Enlisted Members, by Service and IT Group, FY 2002

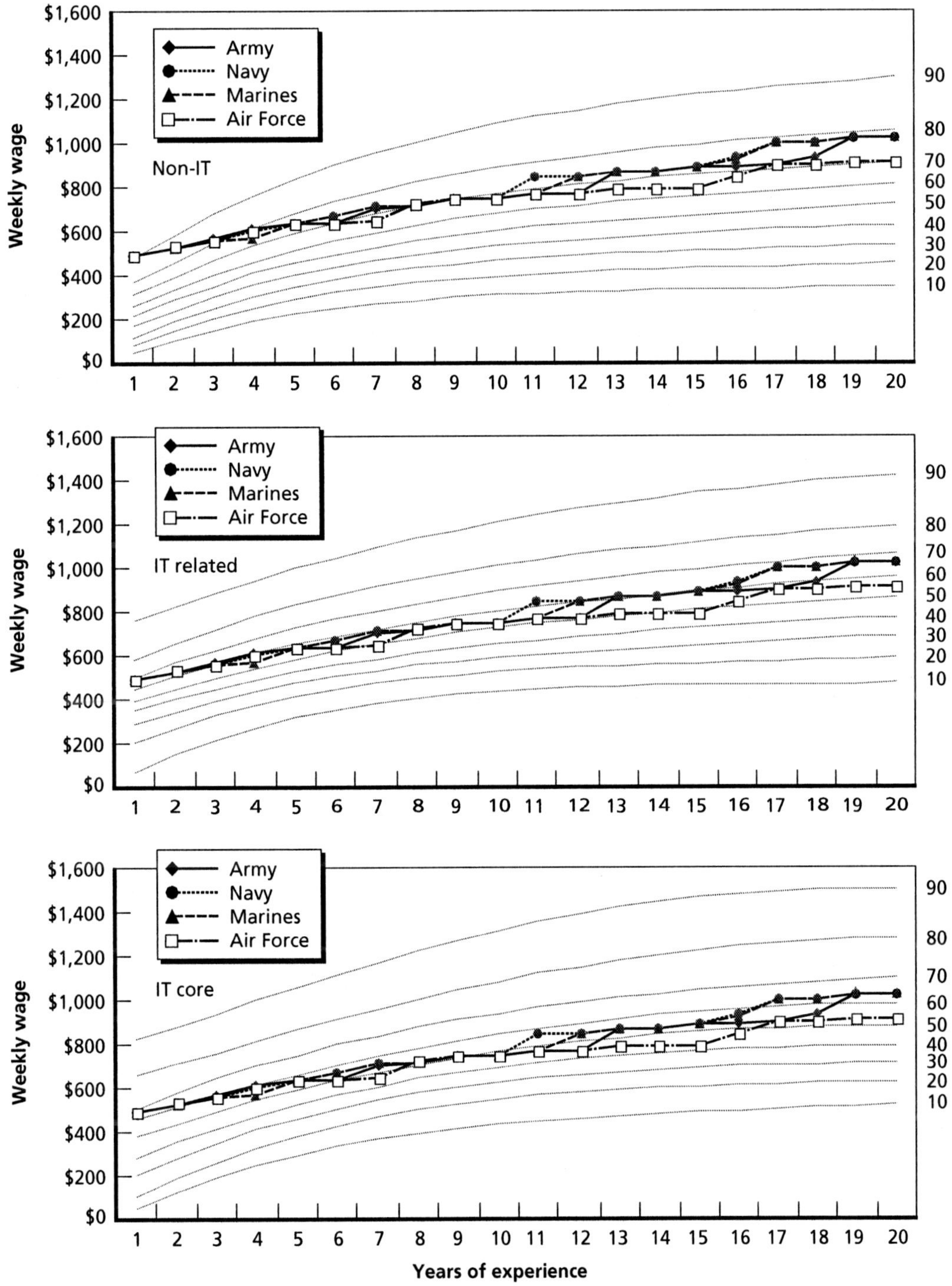

RAND *MG108-5.1*

Figure 5.2
Weekly Civilian Wage Percentiles for Men with Four or More Years of College and Regular Military Compensation for Officers, by Service and IT Group, FY 2002

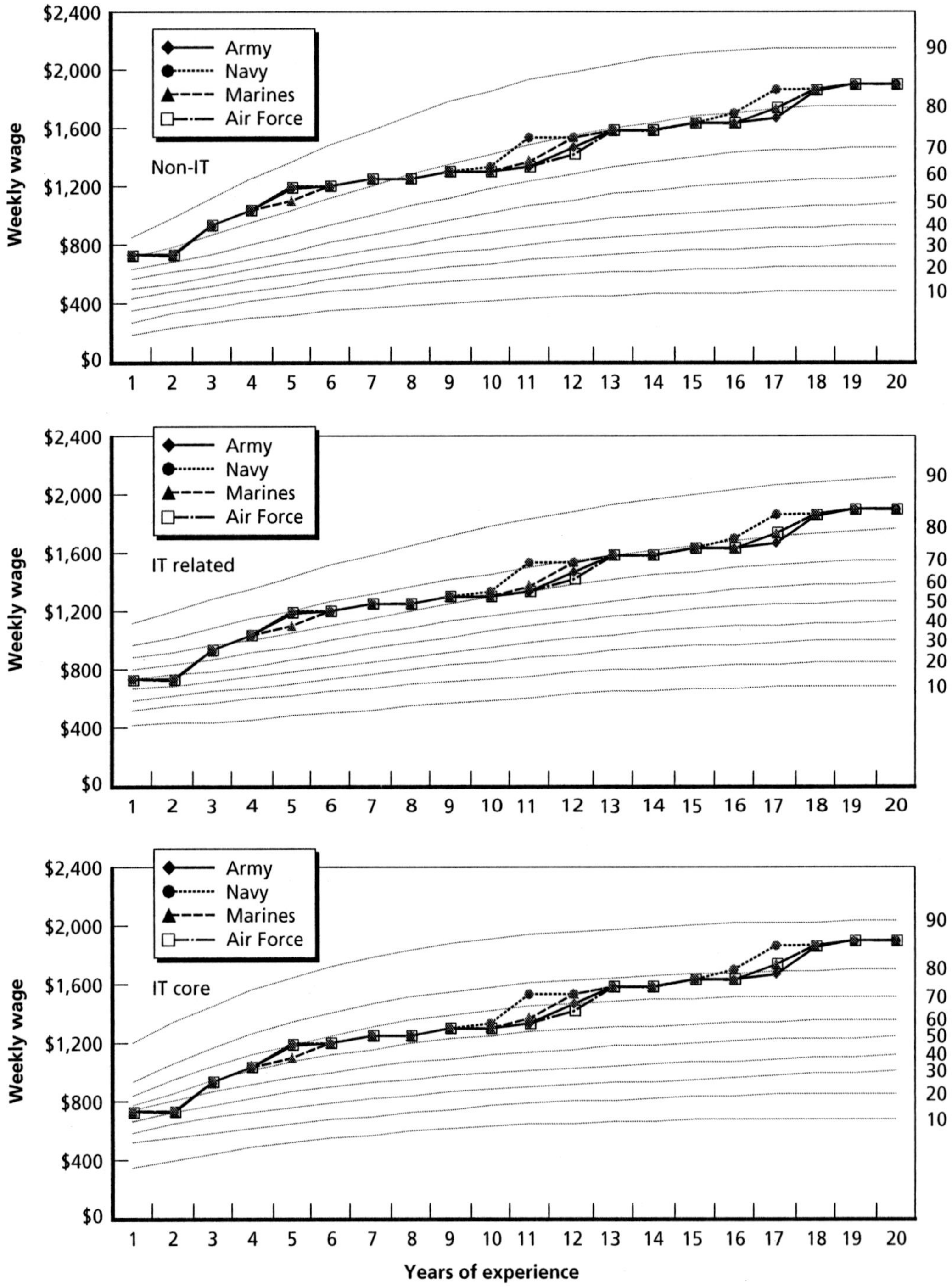

RAND *MG108-5.2*

Figure 5.3
Weekly Civilian Wage Percentiles for Women with Some College and Regular Military Compensation for Enlisted Members, by Service and IT Group, FY 2002

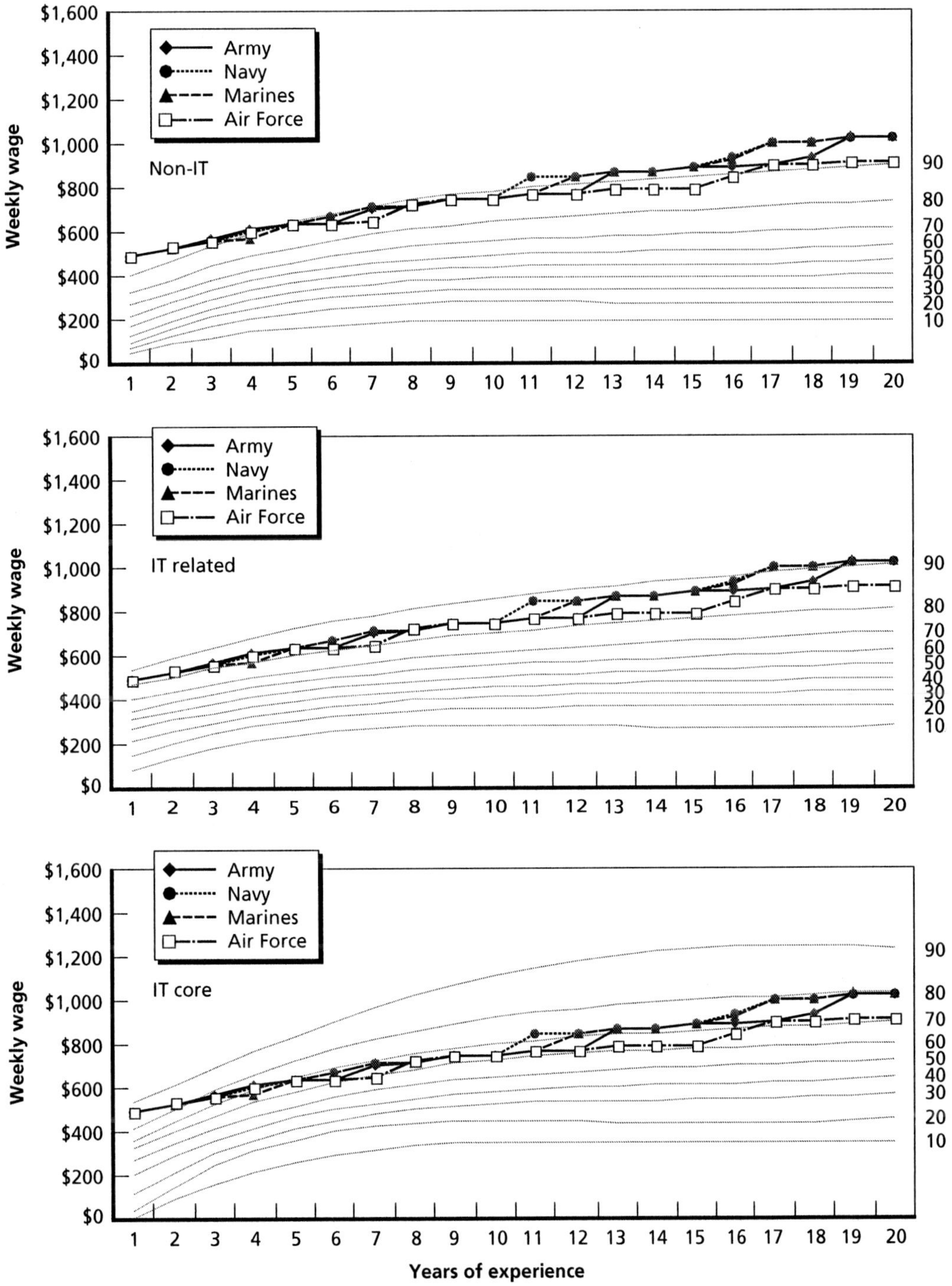

RAND *MG108-5.3*

Figure 5.4
Weekly Civilian Wage Percentiles for Women with Four or More Years of College and Regular Military Compensation for Officers, by Service and IT Group, FY 2002

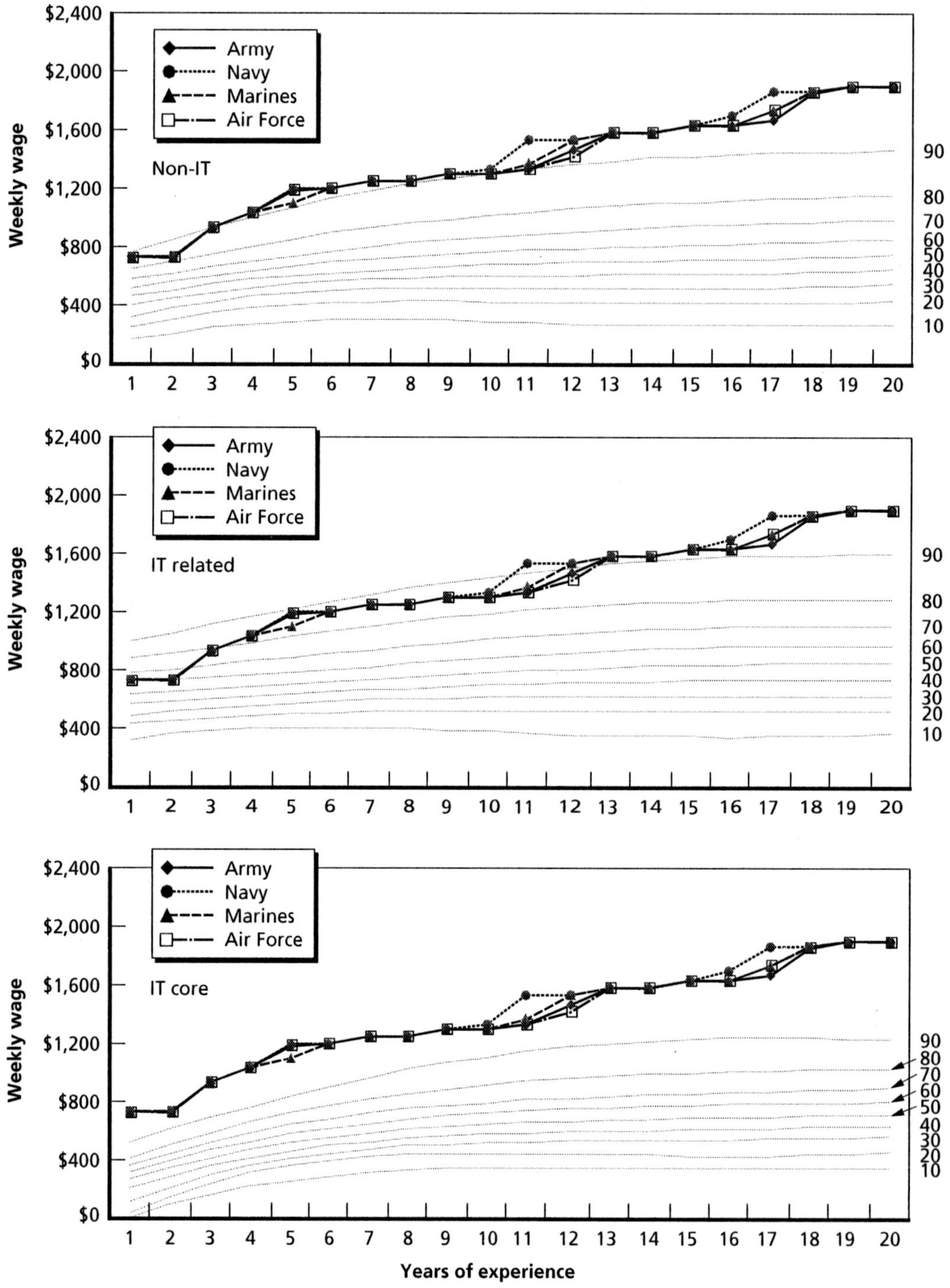

RAND *MG108-5.4*

We conclude from our wage comparisons for women with some college that RMC is lowest relative to the pay in IT-core occupations. RMC is at the 90th percentile of wages in non-IT occupations throughout the range of experience. In contrast, for IT-related occupations RMC lies between the 80th and 90th percentiles, and in IT-core occupations RMC begins at the 80th–90th percentile, falls to the 60th–70th percentile by year 7, and rises to the 70th–80th percentile at year 17. Also, because women's civilian wages are lower than men's, whereas the military pay scale is no different for women than for men, RMC is relatively higher for women than for men.[20] In IT core, for example, starting wages for men have a median value of around $400 and range from near $0 to $800 per week between the 10th and the 90th percentile. Starting wages for women have a median below $300 and a range of $0 to $500 per week.

For women with four or more years of college, RMC is at or above the 90th percentile in non-IT occupations for most years of experience. But in IT-related occupations, RMC begins at the 60th percentile, traverses to the 80th–90th percentile for years 5 through 12, rises to the 90th percentile for years 13–17, and exceeds the 90th percentile for years 18–20. In IT-core occupations, RMC lies *above* the 90th percentile throughout the range of experience, which contrasts with the results for men, where RMC stood lowest, not highest, relative to civilian wages.

Observations

Our nonparametric analysis of wages by occupation group determined that wages for men and women with some college were higher in IT than in non-IT, and therefore that military pay relative to civilian pay was comparatively lower in IT occupations. This pattern also held for men with four or more years of colleges. However, for women with four or more years of college, military pay was relatively lower in IT-related occupations than non-IT occupations, whereas it was higher in IT-core occupations than non-IT occupations. Furthermore, regression estimates indicated that wages for men with less than four years of college remained flat or trended down over the past two decades, while wages for men with four or more years of college trended up and the upward trend was greatest in IT-core occupations. Wage improvements were more pervasive for women. Wages rose for women with high school, some college, or four or more years of college, and the upward trend was greater in IT than non-IT occupations.

This chapter has analyzed in depth the wage differentials between the civilian and military sectors in both IT and non-IT occupations. When combined with the analysis presented in the previous chapter, which looks at the accession, attrition, and reenlistment rates for IT and non-IT personnel, this chapter offers insight into the challenge facing the military in terms of personnel recruitment and at the success it has had in meeting its IT personnel needs. In particular, the observations made in these two chapters suggest that despite the lower wage of military IT careers, individuals are willing to enlist and to enter these fields. For individuals interested in military service, we argue that the advantage of being able to

---

[20] As mentioned, we use recent, service-wide promotion rates in computing RMC by years of service for men and for women.

train in IT makes military service an attractive stepping-stone to a civilian career in IT after military service.

Our argument would be unpersuasive if we had focused only on wage comparisons because, as we have seen, military pay is lower relative to civilian pay in IT than in non-IT. The lower relative pay in IT could be expected to cause poorer recruiting and retention outcomes, or alternatively, the lower pay in IT would need to be supplemented by high enlistment and reenlistment incentives or special pays in order to prevent poorer recruiting and retention outcomes. Indeed, using an approach based on pay comparisons alone, one study concluded that the military would need to offer higher pay to compete for high-tech personnel.[21] While there is truth in that perspective, our work indicates that it is also important to factor in the value of military training, which, we suggest, may operate as a compensating wage differential that can offset some or all of the need to raise pay. Furthermore, outcomes over the period we examined indicate that training provided enough of a compensating differential to enable the military to compete for IT personnel within the current compensation system.

Finally, the analysis thus far sheds light on the issue of retaining experienced IT personnel. Other things held constant, a higher wage differential between civilian and military careers would lead to lower retention. However, as we have seen in earlier chapters, retention in IT occupations is largely comparable to that of non-IT occupations, which would lead us to suppose that other things are not held constant. Possible factors that could explain both the unexpectedly high retention rate and the willingness of individuals to accept relatively lower-paying military IT jobs include bonuses used to compensate for differences in the military and civilian wage streams, and opportunities for further training and experience in IT that can later be applied in civilian jobs. We will explore these ideas about IT recruiting and retention in the following chapter.

---

[21] Golding, Arkes, and Koopman (1999) conclude that to compete for the high-tech sailors required in the future, the Navy should consider shifting to a skill-based pay system.

CHAPTER SIX

Modeling the Supply of IT Personnel

The preceding five chapters—starting with the survey of relevant literature and including the field interviews; the analysis of actual IT personnel accession, attrition, and reenlistment rates; and the comparison of civilian and military wages in IT and non-IT occupations—have contributed to our understanding of the characteristics of the military's IT workforce, the management of IT career fields, and the military's success in weathering the dot-com boom. Our discussions have also presented some surprising observations that somewhat contradict popular wisdom about the powerful draw of private-sector IT jobs and the military's inadequacy to compete with them. For example, our research has shown that despite higher civilian wages in IT than in non-IT occupations, the services have succeeded in attracting high-quality recruits to IT, inducing them to sign up for somewhat longer terms, and keeping their attrition comparatively low. Also, we have found that IT reenlistment was similar to non-IT reenlistment for the Air Force, higher in the Marine Corps, and lower in the Army and the Navy.

As has been argued throughout this report, it appears that the most likely explanation for these empirical patterns is that of a compensating differential deriving from the value of military IT training in post-service jobs. The IT fundamentals taught in the military are presumably transferable to civilian IT jobs, and the wages in those jobs are higher than in non-IT jobs. As a result, a person on the margin between enlisting and not enlisting may be willing to enlist, and accept a somewhat lower wage for a period of time, because of the value of military IT skills in civilian jobs. Transferable, highly valued IT skills would attract high-quality recruits, create an incentive to select or accept longer terms, and inhibit departure while skills are still being learned. Reenlistment would depend on the perceived value of further military IT training and experience and reenlistment incentives.

To more closely examine this hypothesis, we have developed a model that elaborates on this mechanism by combining enlistment, attrition, and reenlistment into a single, cohesive framework. The model, presented in complete detail in Appendix D, accounts for individual differences in the preference for serving in the military (heterogeneous tastes), allows the time path of IT skill acquisition to vary, and allows for the full or partial transferability of military IT skills to civilian jobs. It is important to note that the model also considers the role of the enlistment contract and personnel management practices in limiting attrition and maintaining a relatively stable IT workforce. Using actual retention and wage data to calibrate the model, we can compute the effect of military IT training on the taste distribution of recruits, the evolution of that distribution as recruits stay or depart, the attrition rate, and the reenlistment rate. Furthermore, the model can shed light on some of the questions left unresolved in our earlier literature review. For example, the model, by looking at the role of enlistment contracts, can help us understand the large difference in personnel turnover between civilian jobs and the military. Turnover of 40 percent per year is not uncommon among young full-time workers at private firms, while turnover of 30 percent or so in *three* years is typical of the military.

Although the model can also be further developed to simulate the effect of personnel management and compensation policies on enlistment, attrition, and reenlistment outcomes, we use it here to illustrate the effect of military IT training on enlistment, attrition, and reenlistment. The model shows how the opportunity to obtain IT training acts as an incentive to join the military, and, once the training has been obtained, a possible incentive to leave the military. As a result, the model offers support for our hypothesis that the value of training has contributed to the ability of the services to attract and retain high-quality personnel in IT even though military pay is relatively lower in IT than in non-IT occupations. The model also illustrates how the distribution of preferences for serving in the military differs between the recruit population and the youth population, and how the distribution evolves among retained members as years of service increase. This understanding of individual preferences is significant because it factors centrally into the decision of a potential recruit to enlist and that of an enlisted member to reenlist or leave the military.

In this chapter, we will describe the model briefly and discuss wage functions, enlistment contracts, and factors affecting the individual's willingness to abide by the contract or to breach it. We will then use the model to illustrate our hypothesis that IT training can be a draw to recruiting and early retention.

Dynamic Retention Model with Enlistment

Our model is an extension of the dynamic retention model developed by Gotz and McCall (1984). To their existing model, we have added the decision to enlist and a cost of switching between military and civilian career tracks.

The dynamic retention model is a dynamic programming model of the decision to continue in military service. The dynamic retention model focuses on decisions made by a service member. The value of continuing depends on current military pay, the individual's preference for military service, the effect of one's immediate circumstances—referred to as a "transitory factor" (e.g., satisfaction from the current assignment, location, unit members, commanding officer, deployment, and so forth)—and the present value of the choice during the next period between continuing in the military or leaving to work in the civilian economy. The value of leaving depends on expected civilian wages and the value of military retirement benefits, if any. The dynamic retention model assumes that a person who leaves the military cannot reenter, which is a reasonable assumption for the military. (The military accepts recruits with prior service, but the number of such recruits is quite small, and reentry occurs only in the most junior ranks.) Under this assumption, one of the reasons for staying in the military in the current period is the option to choose whether to continue in the military *next* period or leave then; leaving in this period forecloses that option.

The dynamic retention model provides a rich theoretical framework within which to model, for example, promotion time, compensation structure, special pays, retirement benefits, and up-or-out rules, which require a member to leave the military if the member has not been promoted to a given rank by a given number of years. In considering enlistment within this model, our extended model assumes that in each period, a person who has not been in the military can choose whether to work as a civilian or to enlist. The extended model formally represents this choice through a separate equation representing the decision to enlist or not. The value of continuing as a civilian depends on current civilian pay, the effect of one's immediate circumstances (e.g., satisfaction from the current work, hours of work, wage, work conditions, supervisor, and so forth), and the present value of the choice that can be made at the beginning of the next period between continuing as a civilian or entering the military. As in the original dynamic retention model, the enlistment decision is a Markov decision process embedded in a dynamic program. The model also contains the two equations of the dynamic retention model, one for the monetary benefits, or benefits for short, from remaining in the military and one for the benefits from civilian employment after leaving the military.

The extended model requires two time clocks. One clock keeps track of chronological time, and the other clock keeps track of time in service. Time in service is relevant because the military pay table is defined with respect to time in service. Furthermore, civilian wages depend on effective experience, and a year in the military may not be equivalent to a year of civilian experience. We define effective experience as the sum of years of civilian experience and adjusted years of military experience.

The extended model provides several advantages. First, it is a natural way of accounting for the distribution of preferences for military service in the population at large. The distribution of preferences among entering service members is drawn from that distribution, that is, it is a posterior distribution conditional on the decision to enlist. This linkage can allow us to see how external factors or military policy changes (including recruiting advertising) affect the preference distribution of entering members. In addition, by separately accounting for time as a civilian and time in service, we allow for the possibility that military experience is not a one-to-one equivalent of civilian experience with respect to civilian wages. We show below how the civilian opportunity wage can depend on pace at which IT skills are acquired in service and the transferability of that experience to civilian jobs. Finally, by formally linking the distribution of preferences for those entering service to the distribution in the population at large, we can analyze whether model parameters that fit a population's enlistment rate also fit the retention profile of enlistees.

Our exploratory simulations suggested that parameters fitting the enlistment rate resulted in too high a level of attrition prior to the reenlistment point and too high a level of retention at the reenlistment point. This led us to pursue a fairly close examination of factors affecting a member's incentive to breach the enlistment contract and the service's countervailing actions to limit outflow.

Our focus on the enlistment contract is a departure from previous applications of the dynamic retention model to enlisted retention. Prior work assumed that stay/leave decisions occur only at the end of a term of enlistment (Daula and Moffitt, 1995; Asch and Warner, 1994), in effect ignoring attrition and the factors that affect it. We argue that these factors include a cost to the member of breaching the enlistment contract as well as the cost of the service's efforts to dissuade the member from departing, as discussed below. When these factors are left out, the model far overpredicts first-term reenlistment. When these factors are included, year-to-year probability of staying (nonattrition) and reenlistment both fit well. Thus, the extended model leads to more reasonable predictions of retention for all years and provides a natural way of distinguishing between retention during a contract and retention at the end of the contract, i.e., reenlistment.

Model Structure

To provide necessary background information, we will first describe the structure and assumptions of our model. We assume a person not yet in the military can enter the military in any year, and a person who leaves the military cannot reenter it. In each year, a person is either in the civilian world and has not yet entered the military, in the military, or out of the military and back in the civilian world. In the context of dynamic programming, the value of the post-military program equals the current civilian wage plus the discounted value of the expected value of the optimal program in the next period, either remaining a civilian or entering the military. The value of the military program equals current military pay, plus one's preference for military service, plus the discounted value of the optimal program in the next period, either remaining in the military or leaving. The value of the post-military program equals the stream of civilian wages earned after leaving the military, plus military retirement benefits if any.

Wage Function: A Point of Departure

The civilian opportunity wage function is of particular interest to our analysis because it offers insight into an individual's expected civilian earnings as a consequence of military training. Because we are interested in the attractiveness of military IT occupations, we focus on a person with no IT skills before entering the military. We consider two aspects of military IT training: How much military IT human capital is imparted over what period of time, and how much of this is transferable to civilian jobs?

We model these aspects by assuming that military IT training enables an individual to shift from the non-IT labor market to the IT labor market. The shift is gradual, and we use the following function in describing the transition from the non-IT wage line to the IT wage line:

$$\lambda(\mu,s,\tau)=\frac{1}{1+e^{-\frac{\tau-\mu}{s}}}.$$

Here, τ represents effective years of experience, defined below, and s is a dispersion parameter governing the rate of transition. For instance, if $\mu=3$, then at three years of effective experience the person will be halfway between the non-IT wage line and the IT wage line, i.e., $\lambda=0.5$. If $\mu=4$, then the halfway point is at four years of effective experience. If $s=1$ and $\mu=3$, the person will be 30 percent of the way at $\tau=2$, 50 percent at $\tau=3$, and 70 percent at $\tau=4$. Higher values of s spread the transition over more years. With a smaller value of s, the 30-percent point would be reached a bit later and the 70-percent point a bit sooner.

The person's civilian opportunity wage is a weighted sum of the non-IT and the IT wages:

$$w_\tau=\lambda(\mu,s,\tau)w_{IT}+(1-\lambda(\mu,s,\tau))w_{non-IT}.$$

To illustrate, Figure 6.1 shows the non-IT and IT annual wage lines at the 70th percentile of the civilian wage distribution for males having some college, along with the transition wage line assuming $\mu = 3$ and $s = 1$.

Because not all military IT training may be transferable to civilian jobs, we assume a year of military service counts for a fraction θ of a year of civilian experience. Effective years of experience are defined as $\tau = t + (\theta - 1)y$, where t represents total years of work experience (e.g., age minus years of school minus six) and y represents years of military service. For an individual whose first work experience occurs in the military, years of work experience initially coincide with years of service, so we have $\tau = \theta y$, and after the individual leaves service we have $\tau = (t - y) + \theta y = t + (\theta - 1)y$, which is the same as the formula in the definition.

Figure 6.2 plots the civilian wage line for a person whose first work experience occurs in the military in IT and who departs the military with, alternatively, three, four, five, or six years of service (YOS). The figure assumes that a year of military service in IT is the equivalent 0.80 of a year of civilian experience in IT ($\theta = 0.80$). This assumption is for illustrative purposes. The actual degree of transferability is an empirical question. It could be estimated by collecting information on military IT skill and experience, and on post-service employment, occupation, and wages.

The civilian opportunity wage lines in Figure 6.2 show the combined effect of gaining IT skill in the military and its partial transferability to civilian jobs, followed by the accumulation of experience on a civilian job. The lowest line, shown for comparison, assumes no military IT experience and therefore represents the non-IT civilian wage line. The wage lines for three, four, and five YOS depict a rapid upward shift in the civilian wage, which occurs because of the time path of gaining IT skills in the military. At the values assumed, namely, $s = 1$ and $\mu = 3$, skills are gained rapidly in years three, four, and five, and the civilian opportunity wage line increases accordingly. However, the civilian opportunity wage for

Figure 6.1
Transition from Non-IT to IT Wage Line

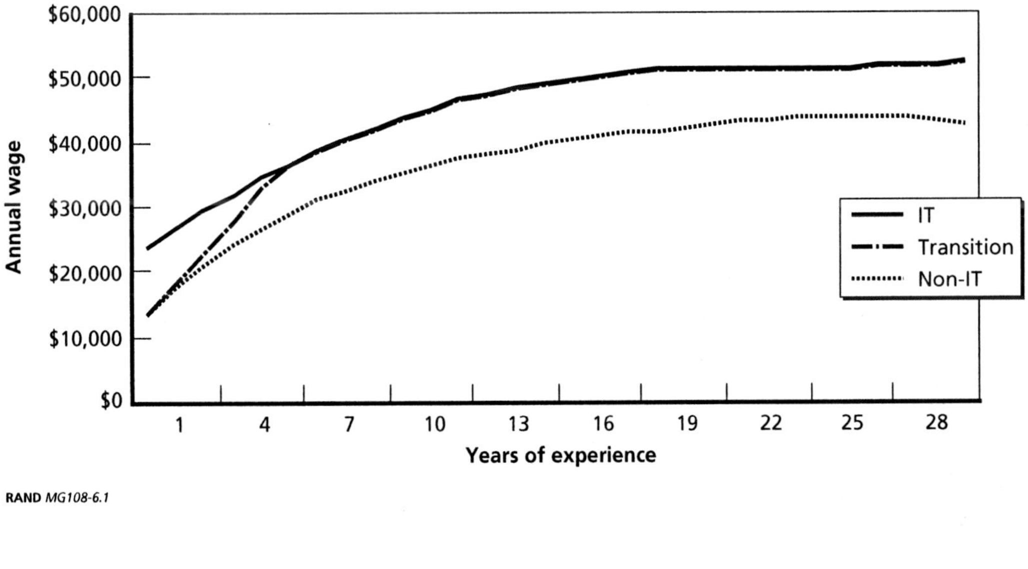

RAND *MG108-6.1*

Figure 6.2
Civilian Opportunity Wage Depends on Transferable Years of Service in Military IT Training

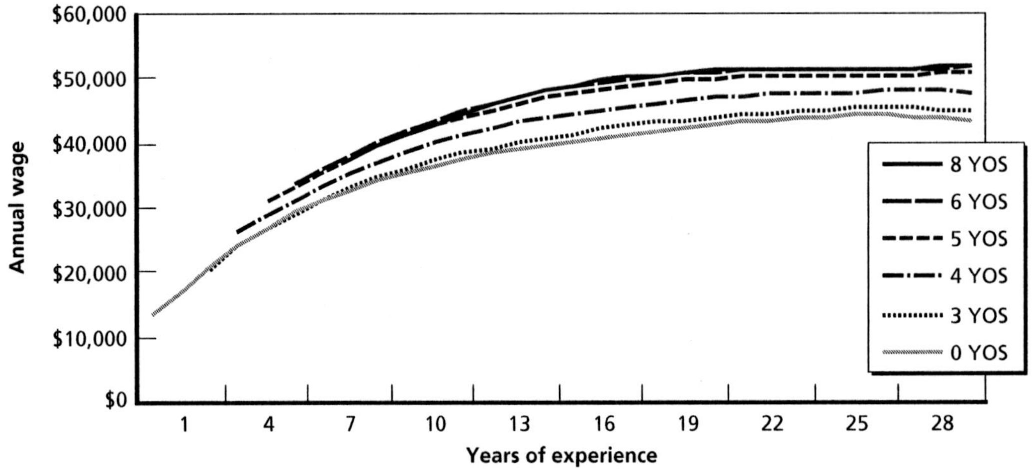

RAND *MG108-6.2*

six YOS is only slightly above the line for five YOS because little additional IT skill is gained in this year and even less in each subsequent year.

A close look at Figure 6.2 shows that the civilian opportunity wage for a person with three YOS in IT is less than the civilian wage at zero years of military service and three years of experience on a non-IT civilian job. The apparent anomaly occurs because IT skill is assumed to grow slowly in the first YOS, and each YOS counts for only 0.8 years of civilian experience. These factors work together to make the civilian opportunity wage slightly lower for a person who entered the military and trained in IT, as compared with a person who worked three years at a non-IT civilian job. But the rapid gain in IT skill in YOS three to five translates into a large increase in the opportunity wage. Here, the wage increase from the gain in IT skill dominates the fact that military experience is not fully transferable. But beyond YOS five IT skills increase slowly, and each YOS continues to be worth only 0.8 civilian years. As a result, the opportunity wage for six YOS is only a bit above that for five YOS, and the opportunity wage for eight YOS is virtually the same as for six YOS.

Whatever one's occupational area (non-IT, IT related, IT core), the value of the military wage stream relative to the civilian wage stream is higher in the initial years of work life. This is because military pay depends only on military experience, not prior civilian experience,[1] and because civilian wages rise with years in the workforce. Military entry pay is the same for someone with one, five, or ten years of civilian experience, but civilian pay is higher for those with more experience. This means the wage incentive to enter the military declines as civilian experience rises.

Moreover, if military experience is not fully transferable, then as we have seen, more years in the military exacts a penalty in the form of civilian wages being somewhat lower than they otherwise would have been. Nevertheless, this penalty may be a small price to pay if

[1] There are some exceptions to this. The entry pay grade for someone with medical skills is E-3, and recruits entering with some college may receive a $4,000 "Hi Grad" bonus in the Army. These exceptions are linked to education rather than job experience.

military training and experience are a gateway to high-paying civilian jobs. From the computations underlying Figures 6.1 and 6.2, we know that the 70th percentile civilian wage for a person with no military experience and five years of civilian experience in a non-IT job is $26,650. If instead the person had four years of military IT experience and one year of civilian experience, the civilian wage would be $28,500 (6.9 percent more than $26,650), and at five years of military IT experience the civilian opportunity wage would be $30,686 (15 percent more). If military IT experience were fully transferable to civilian jobs ($\theta = 1$), the civilian opportunity wage at five years of military IT experience would be $33,128 (24 percent more than the non-IT wage).

Enlistment Contracts

Another essential aspect of our model is the role that the enlistment contract plays in a recruit's decision to enlist and in limiting the attrition rate. To enter service, a recruit must sign an enlistment contract. Since private firms do not demand that new employees sign term contracts, what advantage does the military gain from using a contract? The contract helps the military protect its investment in the recruit's military-specific human capital. The contract is an explicit commitment, entered voluntarily, to serve for a given term. In contrast, the employment-at-will legal doctrine in the civilian economy enables firms to dismiss employees at their discretion, provided their action is fair, nonprejudicial, and based on good-faith efforts to resolve complaints and remediate deficiencies. The military services can dismiss personnel for cause, but the enlistment contract gives the services the privilege of retaining at will, i.e., by signing the contract, a recruit cedes the right to leave at will. Therefore, a service member who wants to leave before the end of the term bears the burden of persuading or inducing the service to agree to a release. Early termination may be made more difficult by the fact that the service may have programs in place to remediate the situation (e.g., if a recruit is overweight or if there is a problem regarding insubordination). We argue that the cost to the member of breaching the contract and terminating service early may be substantial: It may be against the member's self interest; a member leaving without an honorable discharge may bear a cost of switching from the military to the civilian world (beyond the cost of finding a job, which presumably must be borne by anyone leaving the military for civilian work); the member may suffer a loss of anticipated educational benefits and bonus payments and may need to repay prior bonus payments; and the service may act to prevent the member from leaving.

Costs of Breaching

Early Discharge. There are several different reasons for a service member's early discharge. Members who are disruptive, endanger others, disobey orders, abuse drugs, commit acts of violence, and so forth can expect dishonorable or bad-conduct discharges.[2] These discharges occur only if a court martial has convicted the member of a violation of the Uniform Code of Military Justice; conviction is a necessary but not a sufficient condition for these discharges. Other types of early discharge result if the member does not perform adequately,

2 Source: www.usmilitary.about.com/library/weekly/aa092500a.htm. (This and the links listed below were accessed in November 2002).

behaves in a way that brings discredit to the military, or behaves in a way that undermines good order and discipline. It is then up to the member, not the service, to demonstrate that this behavior did not adversely affect the service. Moderately adverse behavior results in a "general discharge under honorable conditions," and significantly adverse behavior results in a "discharge under other than honorable conditions." In the latter, the member will not be eligible for a notice of discharge to employers, which might affect the member's ability to draw unemployment benefits. Members discharged with less than 180 days of continuous active military service are characterized as entry-level separation.

An honorable discharge presumably carries no stigma; an entry-level separation probably has little stigma; but a discharge under other than honorable conditions, a bad-conduct discharge, and a dishonorable discharge are increasingly stigmatic. Early discharge without prejudice can also occur because of injury, physical or mental illness, pregnancy, persistent enuresis, excessive weight, family hardship, or failure to complete basic or advanced individual training. Early discharge with prejudice can occur from infractions of the military code of justice or code of conduct.

Deliberate misbehavior to receive early discharge is not an appealing or truly viable option. In fact, some infractions might lead to imprisonment or disciplinary action rather than early discharge. Furthermore, deliberate misbehavior may exact a psychic cost on the member by violating his or her own ethics. In short, a member's willingness to sign an enlistment contract for a given term of service seems consistent with making a commitment to complete the term if things go as expected, while having the assurance that under certain circumstances the military will allow the member to leave without prejudice. An individual who chooses not to complete his term of service faces costs in a variety of magnitudes and forms.

Self-Interest. The benefits from military IT training may be higher than the benefits from non-IT training, and the benefits from IT training may be higher for high-quality personnel than for non–high quality personnel. Higher benefits from IT than non-IT experience come from the high civilian wage obtainable with additional IT training, which would contribute to lower attrition in IT than non-IT occupations (and fewer breaches of contract). Furthermore, high-quality personnel may learn faster, learn more, and acquire more skill and expertise. With higher benefits from military IT training, the cost of leaving early is also higher. This mechanism, based on individual self-interest, may help explain why high-AFQT personnel have lower attrition in IT, and lower attrition compared with their attrition in non-IT occupations.

Loss of Educational Benefits. The most common enlistment incentives are Montgomery GI Bill educational benefits, "college fund" supplements to the MGIB (the Army College Fund, the Navy College Fund, and the Marine Corps College Fund; the Air Force has no college fund), and bonuses. Members are automatically enrolled for the MGIB when they enter service, and relatively few members choose to dis-enroll. To qualify for the MGIB, the member must be a high school graduate or obtain a GED, contribute $100 a month for 12 months, serve continuously for three years of active duty or serve two years of active duty and four years in the selected reserves, and receive an honorable discharge.[3] The member cannot withdraw funds contributed to MGIB, so if the member leaves after two years but before completing three years and does not enter the selected reserves, the $1,200 is forfeited. MGIB benefits are substantial. The current MGIB rate for a person taking a full load of

[3] Source: www.military.com/Resources/Forms/DD_Form_2366.pdf.

courses is $900 per month for 36 months, a total of $32,400. A member may use MGIB after 24 months active duty but is not fully eligible until completing 36 months of active duty. If the member is discharged prior to reaching 36 months, the member must repay any benefits used.[4]

To qualify for college fund awards, the member must qualify for the MGIB, have an AFQT score of 50 or above, and enlist in a critical specialty offering the college fund.[5] College funds accrue only if the member "obtains and remains qualified for the MOS for which originally enlisted."[6] For instance, the monthly accrual rate for a $12,000 college fund over a three year term is $12,000/36 = $333.

The cost to the member of leaving before 36 months or, having completed 36 months, of leaving without an honorable discharge depends on the accrued benefit to date, the probability of using the benefit, and the expected amount of the benefit that will be used. Many members do not use their educational benefits or use only a portion of them. The accrued benefit is low in the first months of service and continues to rise to the 36th month service. At that point the member is fully eligible. For members eligible for a college fund and having a four-year or longer term, the college fund benefit continues to accrue, with accrual stopping at the end of the fourth year. Therefore, for enlisted members for whom the educational benefit is important, there is significant incentive to remain in the service and complete the agreed-upon term.

Enlistment and Reenlistment Bonus Recoupment. The loss of bonuses is another cost of breaching the enlistment contract. If the member does not satisfy the contractual terms under which the bonus was awarded, the member may be required to repay a portion of the bonus already received.[7] Often, half the bonus is paid at the time of enlistment or reenlistment, and the remainder is paid in equal annual installments on the anniversary dates over the remainder of the term. The recoupment rate equals the total amount of the bonus divided by the number of months in the term. For instance, a $4,800 bonus for a four-year term has a recoupment rate of $100 per month. If the member has served six months of the term, the member has received $2,400 and has "earned" $600 (6 × $100) of the bonus. Therefore, $1,800 ($2,400 – $600) is recouped.[8] In the Army, the maximum enlistment bonus is now $20,000 and the maximum reenlistment bonus is $40,000, up from $12,000 and $20,000, respectively, in 1999.[9] Therefore the cost to the member of breaching the enlistment contract also includes the repayment of bonuses already received and the loss of future bonus installments.

Service Efforts to Limit Outflow. The gain to the service from preventing premature departure is also substantial. Trained, experienced personnel boost military readiness, and by

---

[4] Source: www.news.navy.mil/search/display.asp?story_id=4084.

[5] Source: www.books.usapa.belvoir.army.mil:80/cgi-bin/bookmgr/BOOKS/R621_202/2.14 and www.bupers.navy.mil/pers604/navy%20college%20fund.htm.

[6] Source: www.armyeducation.army.mil/ACF.html#MGIB%20Eligibility%20Criteria.

[7] "A soldier who voluntarily or because of misconduct fails to complete obligated service for which an EB or SRB was paid will refund a percent of the bonus equal to the percent of obligated service not performed." (See www.books.usapa.belvoir.army.mil:80/cgi-bin/bookmgr/BOOKS/R601_280/5.13.)

[8] For other examples, see the following web site: www.osprey.manpower.usmc.mil/manpower/mi/MRA_OFCT.nsf/7366871f85cf0f3e85256a3b006bebbe/136ca9a788fbc17a85256a40004a06b8/$FILE/PadTxt%20ENCL%202.doc.

[9] Table 5.3 contains enlistment and reenlistment bonus prevalence and amount for FY 1999 by service.

reducing attrition, the services reduce the turnover of personnel in units and thereby strengthen unit cohesion. This is especially true in the case of IT occupations, given that these occupations require more extensive technical training and a higher skill base. The enlistment contract provides leeway for the military to control the flow of personnel by allowing for early outs, preventing exits in times of emergency ("stop loss"), promoting qualified personnel to higher ranks as needed, and assigning personnel to designated locations and contingencies. The contract implies that the member will be covered by the Uniform Code of Military Justice, not civil law, and therefore implies that the member is obligated to obey orders. In case of misbehavior, insubordination, or inadequate performance, the member can receive a less-than-honorable discharge, and at the discretion of the service may be court-martialed and deemed ineligible for veteran benefits. The military does not seek compensatory or punitive damages for breach of contract, but glaring offenses can result in imprisonment.

Although the military expects that some recruits will not fit well in the military or will not do well at their specialty, extensive efforts are taken to maintain enlisted personnel in the service until the expiration of their contract. The military may offer remedial physical training, weight control programs, psychological counseling, or the opportunity to change specialty. However, at some point further effort at remediation becomes more costly than separating the member and accessing a new recruit. The service bears the cost of these activities and receives the benefit in the form of "optimized" attrition, i.e., keeping members with good attitudes and performance and separating members with poor attitude and performance, subject to a cost of replacement. For example, if the recruiting command has enlisted members with little willingness to exert effort or with a low preference for military service, the training command may find many of these members unacceptable, resulting in a high rate of attrition.

Adding Breaching Costs And Calibrating the Model

To apply this model to our hypothesis regarding the importance of IT training to the recruitment into and retention of personnel in IT occupations, we needed to calibrate the model and to introduce breaching costs into it. The model was calibrated on each service's retention data. Breaching costs were introduced by subtracting an amount from the civilian wage in the period when the member leaves if that period occurs during the term of the enlistment contract. Including breaching costs enabled the model to generate a close fit with actual retention data, i.e., a good fit with retention prior to reenlistment and after, and a good fit at the reenlistment point. Without breaching costs, the model produced an unacceptably high level of reenlistment and too low a level of probability of staying in other years. We describe and illustrate these results in Appendix D, which also discusses the details of model calibration.

Illustrative Results

Our simulations provided substantial support for the central role of training in the recruitment and retention of IT personnel. The calibration of the model was based on actual retention data and on the non-IT wage line. This was a reasonable approach to calibrating the model because approximately 80 percent of entering personnel are non-IT workers (see Table 4.3 in Chapter Four). The calibrated model produced estimates from which we computed the year-to-year probability of staying in the military and the cumulative retention probability, i.e., the percentage of recruits who are still in the military after a given number of years of service. The calibrated model also identified the distribution of taste for military service among the youth population and among recruits into non-IT occupations.

We then used the parameters calculated for the calibrated model to compute similar values for recruits entering IT occupations. We did this by replacing the non-IT civilian wage line with the IT transition wage line and resolving the model. The baseline (non-IT) model assumed that enlistees were non-IT both before entering service and while in service, and therefore the post-service wage was the non-IT wage given effective years of experience. The IT simulation assumed that enlistees were engaged in non-IT occupations before entering the military but were in IT in service, and the post-service wage was the IT transition wage line given the effective years of experience and the assumed transferability of military IT training. We assumed that the civilian job did not offer further training in IT. This meant that individuals could not leave the military and still have continuity in their IT training. In reality, some employers probably offer training while others do not. The civilian wage depended on the amount of training that had been received at the time of leaving the military, e.g., if an individual progressed 70 percent of the way to the civilian IT wage line, the civilian wage equaled 0.3 of the non-IT wage plus 0.7 of the IT wage, given the individual's effective experience. As mentioned, we chose values of $s = 0.6$, $\mu = 4$, and $\theta = 0.8$, implying that the majority of IT skill acquisition occurred in years two through six and that eight-tenths of military IT skills transferred to civilian IT jobs. Allowing the range of IT learning to continue through year six, the model showed that the military provided some incentive to continue in service at the end of the first term, which was assumed to be four years long.

Effect of IT Training on Civilian Opportunity Wage

In Figure 6.3, we show two lines. The thin line is based on the calibrated non-IT model for the Army and shows year-to-year probability of staying in the military (left panel) and cumulative retention (right panel). We then simulate year-to-year probability of staying in the military for IT training and experience. IT training increases the civilian opportunity wage by enabling the individual to transition from the non-IT civilian wage line to the IT civilian wage line. The individual must weigh the gains from remaining in the military, obtaining further IT training, and thereby increasing the civilian wage obtainable in the future, against leaving the military and opting for the civilian wage obtainable currently. The result (thick line) shows higher year-to-year probability of staying in the years prior to reenlistment than for a member in a non-IT occupation. The IT training is valuable in civilian employment, and the member has an added incentive not to attrite because of that value. The reenlistment decision occurs at the end of a four-year first term, and in this example the reenlistment probability is lower for the IT occupation. At this point, the civilian wage opportunities have already outstripped the combination of military pay and further IT training. The lower reenlistment rate is compensated to some extent by the lower attrition, resulting in similar cumulative retention rates for both IT and non-IT occupations into the second term. This is shown in Figure 6.3. Figures 6.4 and 6.5 show similar simulation results for the Air Force and Navy.

Figure 6.3
Year-to-Year Probability of Staying and Cumulative Retention for Non-IT and IT: Army

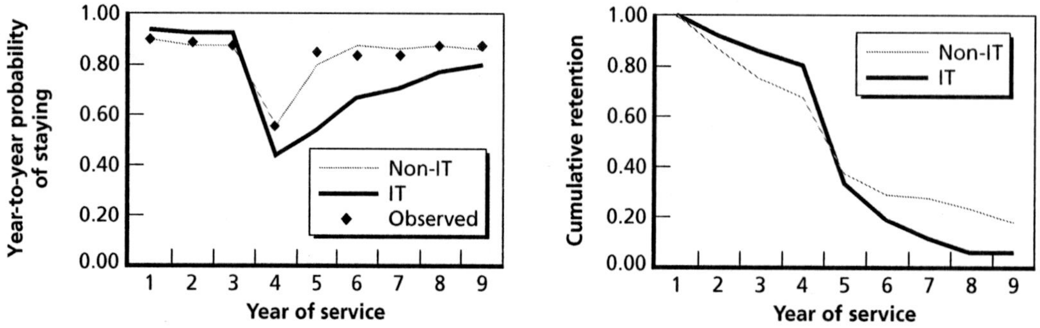

RAND *MG108-6.3*

Figure 6.4
Year-to-Year Probability of Staying and Cumulative Retention for Non-IT and IT: Air Force

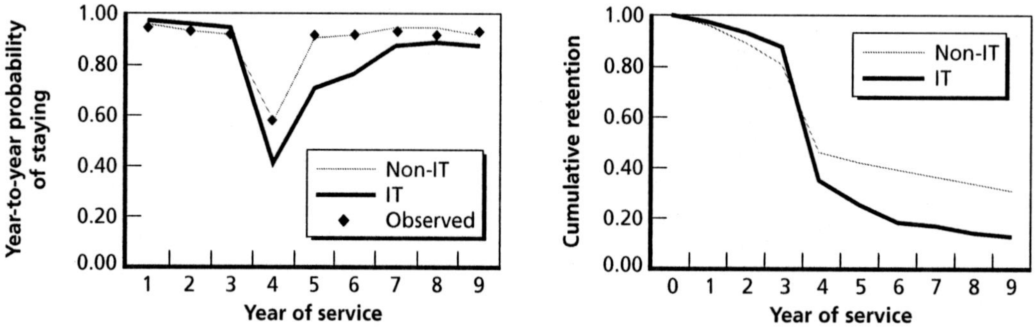

RAND *MG108-6.4*

Figure 6.5
Year-to-Year Probability of Staying and Cumulative Retention for Non-IT and IT: Navy

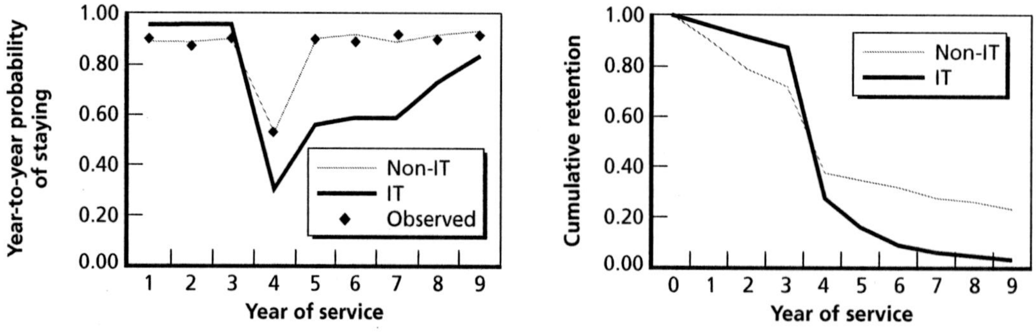

RAND *MG108-6.5*

In addition to higher initial retention, the simulations also showed higher initial enlistment rates for the IT occupations relative to non-IT occupations. The increases are large: a 51 percent increase over the baseline for the Army, 43 percent for the Air Force, and 100 percent for the Navy. Although the simulation does not differentiate among individuals by their quality (e.g., AFQT score), the large increase in enlistment is a measure of the attractiveness of military IT compared with non-IT. This means that more potential recruits would be drawn to IT, and the services would have a larger number of high-quality candidates to choose from. Furthermore, although the simulation does not allow the civilian IT wage to depend on quality, this could be done. As discussed in Chapter Four, it seems likely that the gains from IT training are higher for high-quality individuals, and if so, the higher civilian opportunity wage would be another factor explaining why military IT has been successful in recruiting high-quality personnel and keeping their attrition low.

The simulations show how military IT training serves as a compensating differential to assist recruiting and early retention in IT. The members in IT occupations show a higher enlistment rate, and a lower attrition rate, due to the value of future military IT training. However, members in IT occupations are also more difficult to retain once they have completed their training. In the simulation, much of the training was completed by the fourth year of service, resulting in the need to provide higher retention bonuses to keep reenlistment rates up for these occupations. However, if training extended well into the second term, the value of that training would increase first-term reenlistment and reduce the need for a reenlistment bonus. Depending on the value of IT training in the second term, IT reenlistment could be higher than non-IT reenlistment even without a bonus.

We next present graphics for the distribution of preferences for military service in the youth population compared with entering members, and the evolution of that distribution among retained members.

Prior and Posterior Taste Distributions

Figures 6.6–6.8 show the calibrated distribution of taste prior to joining one of the services and the distribution of taste for those who decide to enter one of the services. The distribution of taste among youth was assumed to be extreme-value distributed, with a long right-hand tail. We refer to this *prior* distribution of taste for service among the youth population as the "youth" distribution. We assume this distribution is the same regardless of whether a youth subsequently entered an IT occupation or a non-IT occupation in the military. We compute the *posterior* distribution of taste among new entrants as the prior distribution conditional on choosing to enlist. We call this the "non-IT recruit" distribution for personnel entering non-IT occupations, and the "IT recruit" distribution for those entering IT occupations. The non-IT recruit computation employs the non-IT civilian wage line, while the IT recruit computation employs the IT transition civilian wage line.

The model calibration led to fitted values of the taste distribution with a modal value of tastes at –\$16,000 for the Army and the Air Force and –\$13,000 for the Navy. The negative taste in the youth population is a reflection of the demanding, risky nature of military service relative to civilian career paths. The negative modal taste goes hand in hand with the fact that the military must pay an above average level of compensation. As seen in Chapter Five, military pay for non-IT positions is approximately the 70th percentile of civilian pay. But the figures also show that the modal taste of those volunteering to enter military service is several thousand dollars higher. The military pay premium represents the amount the military must pay to meet its accession targets given the mechanism of self-selection into the military.

Figure 6.6
Distribution of Taste for Military Service in Youth Population and Among Recruits: Army

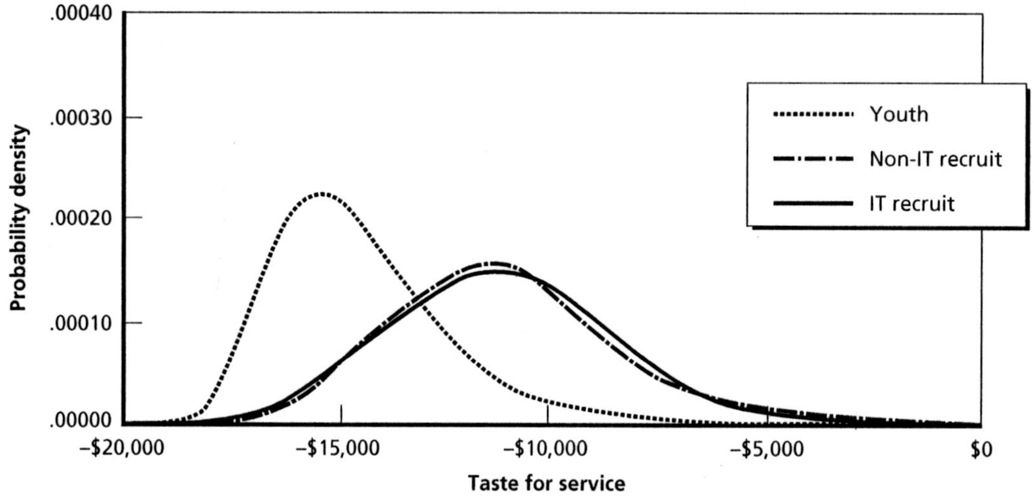

RAND *MG108-6.6*

Figure 6.7
Distribution of Taste for Military Service in Youth Population and Among Recruits: Air Force

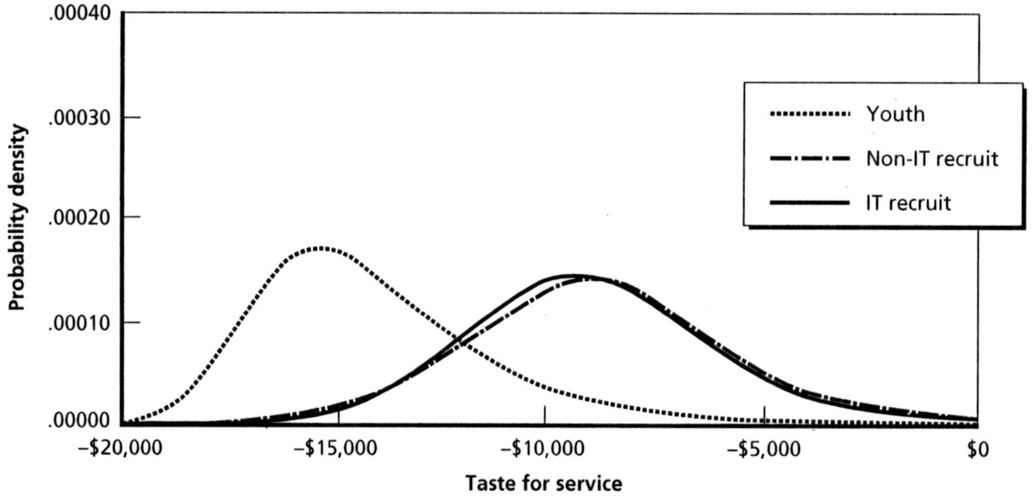

RAND *MG108-6.7*

Figure 6.8
Distribution of Taste for Military Service in Youth Population and Among Recruits: Navy

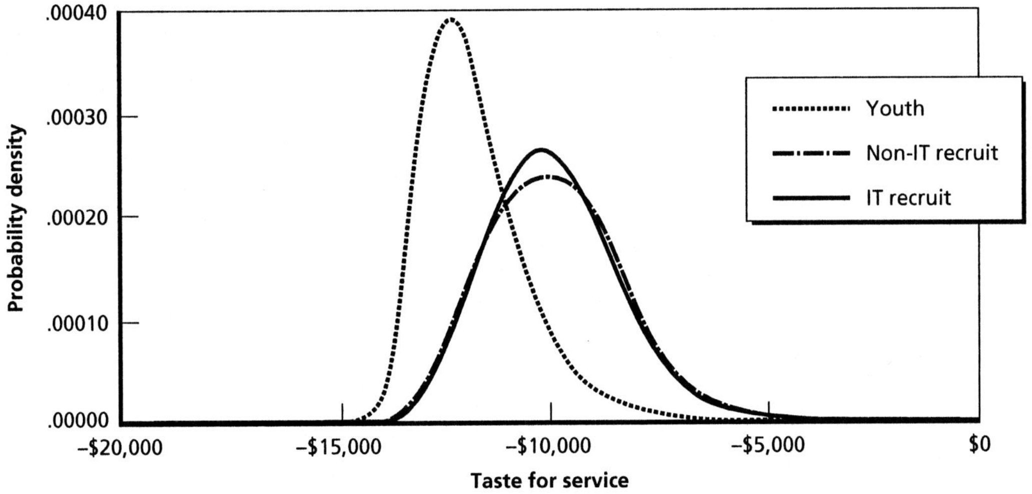

RAND *MG108-6.8*

Furthermore, this is true both for recruits entering non-IT occupations and for those entering IT occupations. As seen, their taste distributions are fairly similar. The modal taste is about –$11,500 for Army recruits, –$9,000 for Air Force recruits, and –$10,000 for Navy recruits.[10] However, as we will see below, the mean taste of recruits entering IT is less than that of recruits entering non-IT. The explanation is that because of the value and transferability of military IT training, recruits with a lower taste for military service are willing to enlist into IT occupations.

Evolution of the Taste Distribution over Time

As enlistees separate from the military, the distribution of taste for military service for the people who remain changes. This is because individuals with a lower taste have a higher propensity to leave. The upper two panels in Figures 6.9–6.11 show how the taste distribution changes by year of service in non-IT and IT occupations. The left-most distribution is the distribution at the beginning of the first year of service. At this point, service members have served for one year.[11] The lighter curves show the taste distribution for successive years of service. Because we assumed a four-year term length, a comparison of the distributions for years four and five indicates how the distribution is affected by the outflow of personnel at the reenlistment decision point. We see that the taste distribution generally shifts to the right as years of service increase, and the shift is more pronounced at reenlistment.

---

[10] Also, the distribution looks symmetric. This suggests that assuming a normal taste distribution in a dynamic retention model would be a good choice. The dynamic retention model focuses on individuals who are already in the military. The studies by Daula and Moffitt (1995) and Asch, Johnson, and Warner (1998) in fact assumed normality.

[11] This is the same numbering convention as commonly used in keeping track of birthdays. For instance, a five-year-old has completed five years since birth and is in his sixth year of life.

Figure 6.9
Taste Distribution and Mean Taste by Year of Service: Army

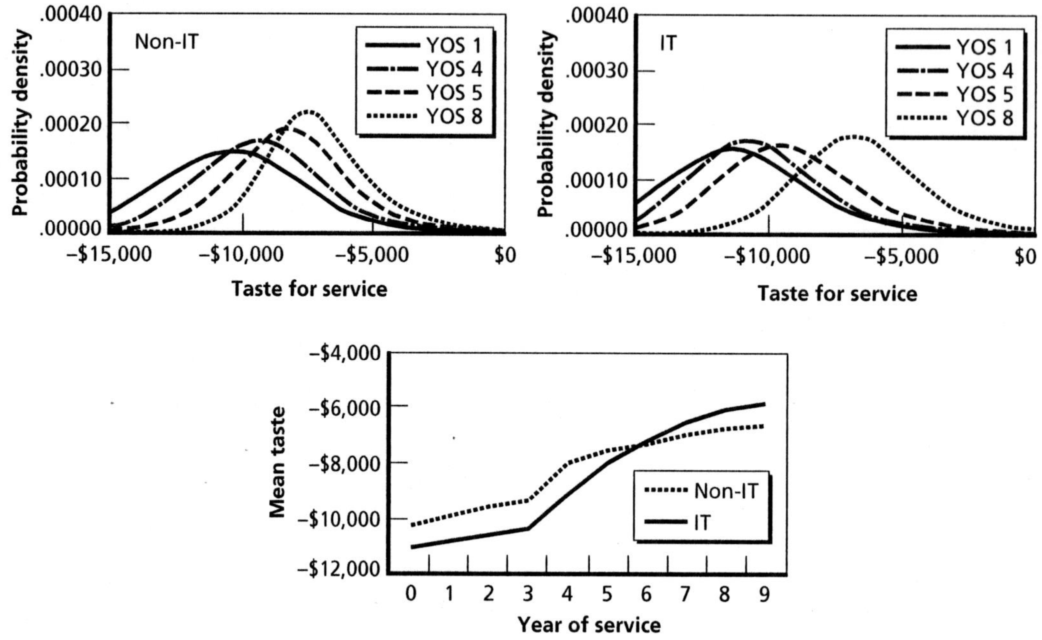

RAND *MG108-6.9*

Figure 6.10
Taste Distribution and Mean Taste by Year of Service: Air Force

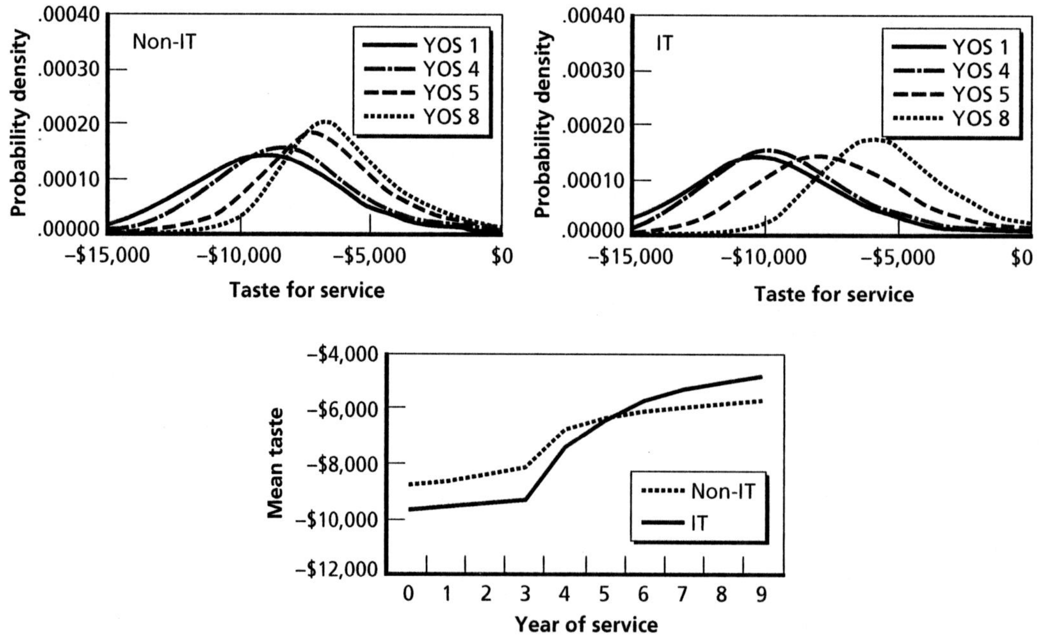

RAND *MG108-6.10*

Figure 6.11
Taste Distribution and Mean Taste by Year of Service: Navy

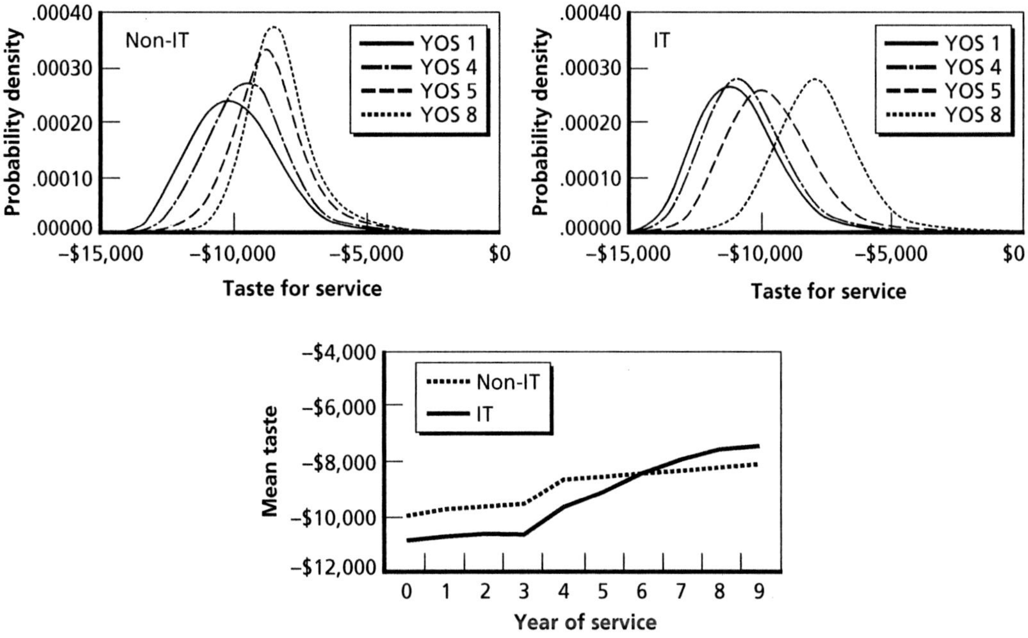

RAND *MG108-6.11*

The lower panel in the figures shows how the mean taste changes as years of service increase. It rises by several thousand dollars over the first nine years of service, and it increases rapidly at first-term reenlistment as members with a higher taste tend to stay and those with a lower taste tend to leave. But the change in mean taste differs between IT and non-IT. As mentioned, the mean taste at entry is somewhat lower (about $1,000 lower) in IT than in non-IT. This difference persists during the first term. It persists because of the cost of breaching the enlistment contract, which is felt by personnel in IT and non-IT alike, and because of the greater incremental value of remaining in service to acquire more IT training and experience, relative to the higher civilian wage commanded by IT training already acquired.

This situation changes at the time of first-term reenlistment. Although significant gains from further IT training continue into the fifth year of service under our assumed training profile, much of the training has been completed by the fourth year. For some IT personnel, the gains from remaining in service are not large enough relative to the gains of leaving. These will tend to be personnel with a lower taste for military service, i.e., the same type of personnel who were, on the margin, induced to enlist in the military for IT training in the first place. In fact, the pull of civilian wage opportunities now works against IT occupations: By the time six years of service have been completed, the mean taste of personnel remaining in IT becomes *greater* than the mean taste of personnel in non-IT.

Again, these results are illustrative and depend on assumptions about the value and transferability of military IT training. The results would differ under different assumptions. For example, if we assumed that all transferable IT training was provided in the first three years of service, there would be no training-related reason to reenlist for a second term. If we assumed that transferable training was provided throughout the second term, there would be a strong reason to reenlist. Thus, the theory and simulated results indicate how the value of training can make a difference in enlistment, attrition, and reenlistment, and further, how it can affect the mean taste for military service among those serving.

Closing Thoughts

Because of its design, its incorporation of additional variables, and its application to IT personnel and training, our model is a useful extension of the dynamic retention model. By showing how military IT training can attract individuals who otherwise would not have joined the military, the model demonstrates how IT increases the supply of prospective recruits and thereby enables the services to be more selective in channeling recruits into IT.

The model and simulations reflect some key characteristics of personnel supply in IT occupations. The members in IT occupations show a lower attrition rate, because of the value of future training. Members in IT occupations are also more difficult to retain, because of their higher opportunity wage, resulting in the need to provide continued training (i.e., career growth opportunities) or higher retention bonuses to keep reenlistment rates up for these occupations. Most important, the results of our analysis are able to explain the unexpected data for IT personnel flows, recruitment, attrition, and retention rates that we described in Chapter Four and the conflict between these data and the wage differential outlined in Chapter Five. The model depicts a mechanism through which training acts as an effective and appealing incentive that has allowed the military to compete successfully for IT personnel.

CHAPTER SEVEN

Conclusion

Our work was motivated by the question of whether the military was vulnerable to future shortages in IT personnel. Our net assessment is that because of the civilian sector value of IT skills learned during military service, the IT occupations in the armed forces have been able to attract higher-quality recruits, for longer first terms, and with lower attrition rates than the non-IT occupations. In addition, the IT retention rates have been similar to those in non-IT occupations. This perspective views IT training as a form of compensation that in part counterbalances the lower military/civilian wage ratio in IT compared with non-IT. It is important to note that we classified IT occupations into IT-core and IT-related occupations, the latter of which also includes many high-tech occupations. Therefore, the role of military IT training may be one that extends beyond IT training per se and includes other valuable, transferable skills. If so, the importance of IT training in securing the supply of IT personnel is part of a broader fabric in which military training is an important component in attracting high-quality personnel and channeling them into high-skill areas.

In framing our research, we also wanted to know whether the services had mapped out a path between IT personnel supply and management policies at present and IT manpower requirements in the future. This led us to differentiate between long-term visions of future force structures and doctrines and nearer-term processes to identify manpower requirements. It was perhaps not surprising to find that long-term visions do not serve the role of identifying specific resource requirements, manpower or otherwise. However, the nearer-term processes for determining resource requirements are more well defined. These processes assist the services in considering resource trade-offs, developing budget submissions, determining resource allocations to each unit within a command, and developing appropriate training and skill development programs. Furthermore, it is our sense that as new systems phase in, the planning horizon is typically long enough to permit these processes to work effectively. Our look into the requirements determination processes was limited, however, and we did not analyze whether the processes led to the most cost-effective resource requirements or whether their flexibility and responsiveness could be improved. Nevertheless, the services can and do use the processes to specify emerging manpower requirements, and the very near-term requirements are used in assigning personnel to positions (faces to spaces).

Our conclusions are most relevant to the current defense environment and the existing planning procedures. We would expect that given no major departures from past experience, the observations and implications that we have drawn from our research about the services' ability to attract recruits into IT and retain them at reasonable rates should continue to be applicable, enabling the services to meet future IT manning requirements. However, a large increase in the authorized size of the active duty force could cause a sharp increase in the demand for new and experienced IT (and other) personnel. Also, a decline in the value of

IT skills in the civilian economy would reduce the attractiveness of military IT training. In these cases, adding enlistment incentives, reenlistment incentives, and special pays could help to secure the supply of IT personnel.

Meeting Active Duty IT Manpower Requirements

Attractiveness of Military IT Specialties

This report has shown that, contrary to our expectations, the military has been able to recruit high-quality personnel into IT occupations and induce them to sign on for longer terms. In fact, the percentage of recruits who were high quality was higher in IT occupations than in non-IT occupations, as was the percentage of recruits who signed on for longer terms. This occurred without offering more or larger enlistment bonuses to IT personnel. Furthermore, attrition rates in IT occupations were lower than those of non-IT occupations, and retention rates were mixed.

These results led us to ask the question, Why were high-quality recruits willing to enter IT and sign on for longer initial terms? We hypothesized that recruits saw IT providing an edge over other military specialties because its training and experience were a pathway to high-paying careers after military service. Recruits, all of whom by definition had a preference for military service, apparently perceived a significant post-service value from a military IT occupation. The incentive was strong enough to induce them to choose a long term if need be, i.e., if only long terms were offered or if all shorter-term positions had already been filled at the time the recruit was signing up. Consistent with the high value of IT training and experience, IT recruits had lower attrition. This was not just a reflection of the well-known fact that high-aptitude recruits have lower attrition in general; our results indicated that, at a *given* aptitude, attrition was lower in IT than non-IT. Moreover, the value was higher for high-aptitude recruits; as fast learners, they could expect to build more IT human capital and had a greater incentive to enter IT.

Taken on its own, our hypothesis that the value of training is responsible for the higher quality and lower attrition of IT recruits might suggest that reenlistment of IT personnel would also be lower, since they were more likely to seek higher-paying civilian-sector jobs following completion of their training. But as noted above, the reenlistment picture was mixed. Reenlistment was lower in IT than in non-IT in the Army and the Navy, about the same in the Air Force, and higher in IT in the Marine Corps. The use of reenlistment bonuses no doubt influenced these outcomes.[1] In addition, whatever the effect of bonuses, a member's willingness to reenlist also may have been influenced by the value of further military training and experience in IT in the second term of service and beyond.

The theoretical framework we developed proved powerful in unifying these ideas. Our model calibration and simulations demonstrated that under reasonable assumptions, the value of military IT training for civilian jobs would serve to increase enlistment and reduce attrition. The higher potential enlistment could enable the services to enlist higher-quality recruits into IT and induce them to sign on for longer terms. Also, depending on the use of

[1] The percentage of personnel receiving reenlistment bonuses was higher in IT in the Army, the Navy, and the Marine Corps but lower in the Air Force. Bonus amount differed little between IT and non-IT in the Army, but was higher in IT in the Navy and the Marine Corps and a bit higher in IT in the Air Force.

reenlistment bonuses and the value of military IT training beyond the first term, the model could generate similar or even higher reenlistment in IT than in non-IT.

Adapting to Compete with the Private Sector

The findings of this report imply that the military is actually well suited to compete with private-sector firms for high-aptitude individuals at the entry level in IT. As we described in our survey of academic and popular literature, people commonly believed at the end of the 1990s that private-sector employers offered IT workers high wages, flexible work schedules, access to new hardware and software, and ample training to stay up-to-date. Private-sector job classification and assignment were fluid and responsive in comparison with the military and civil service. In contrast, the military compensation system was seen by some as inflexible because it did not allow pay to differ by occupation.

Although private-sector employers were painted in the popular press as being hyper-responsive to the needs of IT workers, we found little rigorous evidence to document the investment and adaptation actually being made. The description in the press seemed more based on anecdote, fad, and surveys that were not random, rather than on what was in fact being done. Certainly, some employers adapted to the pressures of the dot-com era by offering new equipment, ample training, flexible schedules, and so forth, but many employers of IT workers are not cutting-edge IT users, and we found little documentation that these supposedly "best practices" were widespread.

At the same time, our interviews with military officials in the Army and the Air Force, documented in Chapter Three, revealed that the services had fairly sophisticated resource requirement assessment and generation techniques in place during the 1990s and had taken steps to update and streamline their IT personnel management systems.[2] We learned in field interviews that the military had reclassified positions to emphasize their reliance on IT and made it easier for service members to obtain additional training and education while in service. The military also offered certification in IT skills. Still, there were no military incentives, such as faster promotion or special pay, for obtaining additional training and education, and some of those we interviewed believed that IT education and training contributed to lower retention.

Existence of a Manpower Planning Process

Regardless of the exact number and nature of IT occupations in the future military, it seems clear that future force structures will rely heavily on IT for advanced intelligence and integrated command, control, and communication. But this is not new. The movement toward more and more-advanced IT has gone on for decades, and IT in future forces will not be an abrupt, discontinuous jump from the past. The services already have planning groups in place to define the manpower and training requirements of new systems as they phase in. Although IT manpower requirements are not precisely defined in distant future force structures, having a planning process with planning cycles long enough to allow manpower to adjust can prevent a serious deficiency. The current system uses a planning cycle that affords

---

[2] Civil service has reduced the number of job classifications, created broader pay bands, introduced limited forms of pay for performance, and increased time for ongoing training. Furthermore, flexible legislation has allowed the GAO to implement special, higher pay rates for civilian employees, in order to attract qualified, entry-level individuals (see www.gao.gov/new.items/d011007t.pdf, last accessed November 2003).

time enough to change accession requirements, training programs, and personnel classification and to meet the manpower requirements of the new system. In fact, an overly exact planning process could limit innovation and creativity in the long run. The IT manpower requirements materialize through the process of research, development, testing, and evaluation, which is often years long and which can evolve as technologies are invented and applied. As the capabilities and parameters of new systems become clearer, manpower planners can be more confident and specific about the appropriate timetable, experience mix, training, and quality/aptitude requirements. In addition, because future force structures are visions, the lack of specificity in manpower requirements is not surprising; a specific statement of requirements would not be credible, or at best it would have a wide margin of error.

The manpower planning process, however, does not eliminate the need for the development of a process that can conduct broader reviews of personnel force structure and compensation and that can address questions outside the purview of the process. Such questions include whether careers should be lengthened and where, e.g., should junior and early-career personnel stay longer and should personnel with over 20, or 30, years of service stay longer? Should career tracks be reengineered, e.g., should the United States create cadres of exceptionally talented IT personnel in order to accelerate within-service process innovation in combat and support activities, just as the Israeli Army has developed its highly innovative computer corps? Given the emphasis on innovation and creativity in the current transformation of the military, it may be valuable to define and evaluate, by field demonstration, alternative resource configurations along with the development of metrics to measure their effectiveness.

A Challenge: Improving Data for Policy Analysis

Our research has provided insight into the supply of IT personnel; however, it has done little to assess IT manpower requirements. While our findings offer some confirmation that recruiting and retention in IT are adequate to meet current IT manpower requirements, the defense manpower research community lacks data to assess whether the requirements—or IT enlistment and retention targets—are optimal. The detailed information, data, and models used in the derivation of manpower requirements are typically unavailable to the defense manpower research and policy communities. Also lacking are data on the productivity of IT personnel, the underlying factors determining productivity, the value of additional experience in IT, and the optimal experience mix of IT personnel.

Personnel data could also be improved by including information on the use of bonuses and educational benefits. This information was absent from our personnel data, although it is available in pay files. Had these data been routinely integrated into the personnel files, we could have tracked bonus and benefit prevalence and award amounts. Similarly, we did not have data on educational benefit usage while members are in service or after service. Also, it is hard to find data on military IT career opportunities and how they compare with post-service, private-sector IT employment and earnings. We therefore know little about how military personnel would respond to various types of improvements in career opportunities. Given the almost certain importance of IT occupations and capabilities of the future armed forces, these issues seem to be potential candidates for policy attention and future study.

APPENDIX A

Military and Civilian IT Occupations Used in This Report

The IT-core occupations in the military were designated as such in a Pentagon study of information assurance and information technology personnel (U.S. Office of the Secretary of Defense, 1999). Because there is no accepted taxonomy of IT occupations, the IT-related occupations in the military (as well as the civilian IT-core and IT-related occupations) were selected on the authors' best judgment. The IT-core occupations include computer programmer, operator, systems designer, scientist, operations researcher and analyst, peripheral equipment operator, and electrical and electronic technician. IT-related occupations are intended to include occupations where information technologies are integral to the performance of tasks required by the job. IT-related occupations in the military include radio, radar, and sonar operator; navigation, surveillance, air traffic control, and combat operations; various intelligence and signal occupations; fire control systems; mapping; analysis; and others. IT-related occupations in the private sector include occupations such as electronic repair and communications operator, computer-numerically controlled machine operator, telephone operator, calculating machine operator, air traffic controller, bookkeeper, accounting and auditing clerk, architect, scientist, financial analyst, and others.

Table A.1
IT Core, Military

Occupation	DoD Occupation Code
Communications radio[a]	101
Navigation/communication/countermeasures[a]	102
ADP computers/general	150
Teletype and cryptographic equipment/generation	160
Training devices[e]	191
Shipboard inertial navigation systems	193
Electronic instruments/n.e.c.	198
Radio code[d]	201
Communications center operations/general	260
Operator/analyst	531
Programmer	532
Functional analysis[c]	558
Wire communications/general[b]	620
Lineman	621
Central office	622
Interior communications[e]	623

NOTES: n.e.c. is "not elsewhere classified." Military occupations include all services except as noted.
[a]Navy only.
[b]Army and Marines only.
[c]Air Force only.
[d]Air Force and Navy.
[e]Navy, Air Force, and Marines.
[f]Air Force, Marines, and Army.
[g]Army and Navy.

Table A.2
IT Core, Civilian

Occupation	Census Occupation Code
Computer systems analyst and scientist	64
Operations and system researcher, analyst	65
Computer science teacher	129
Electrical and electronic technician	213
Broadcast equipment operator	228
Computer programmer	229
Tool programmer, numerical control	233
Supervisor, computer equipment operators	304
Supervisor, financial records processing	305
Computer operator	308
Peripheral equipment operator	309

Table A.3
IT Related, Military

Occupation	DoD Occupation Code
Navigator[e]	61
Radio/radar/general	100
Communications radio[f]	101
Navigation/communication/and countermeasures[f]	102
Air traffic control radar[e]	103
Surveillance/target acquisition and tracking	104
Bomb navigation[c]	111
Airborne fire control[d]	112
Shipboard and other fire control	112
Missile guidance and control[g]	113
Missile checkout equipment/test equipment	121
Sonar/general	122
Radio code[g]	130
Non-code radio	201
Sonar operator/general[d]	202
Radar	210
Air traffic control	221
Signal intelligence/electronic warfare[a]	222
Intercept operator (code and non-code)	230
Analysis	231
Electronic countermeasures	232
Operational intelligence	233
Counterintelligence[g]	243
Combat operations control/general	244
Medical administration and logistics	250
Mapping[g]	340
Surveying	411
Drafting[g]	412
Illustrating	413
Other technical specialist and assistance[d]	414
Administration/general	496
Auditing and accounting	541
Precision equipment/general	670

NOTE: Military occupations include all services except as noted.
[a]Navy only.
[b]Army and Marines only.
[c]Air Force only.
[d]Air Force and Navy.
[e]Navy, Air Force, and Marines.
[f]Air Force, Marines, and Army.
[g]Army and Navy.

Table A.4
IT Related, Civilian

Occupation	Census Occupation Code
Financial manager	7
Accountant and auditor	23
Other financial officer	25
Management analyst	26
Architect	43
Aerospace	44
Metallurgical and materials	45
Mining	46
Petroleum	47
Chemical	48
Nuclear	49
Civil	53
Agricultural	54
Electrical and electronic	55
Industrial	56
Mechanical	57
Marine and Naval architect	58
Engineer, n.e.c.	59
Surveyor and mapping scientist	63
Actuary	66
Statistician	67
Mathematical scientist, n.e.c.	68
Physicist and astronomer	69
Atmospheric and space scientist	74
Industrial engineering technician	214
Mechanical engineering technician	215
Engineering technician, n.e.c.	216
Drafting occupations	217
Surveying and mapping technician	218
Air traffic controller	227
Chief communications operator	306
Supervisor; distribution, scheduling, and adjusting clerk	307
Bookkeeper, accounting, and auditing clerk	337
Billing, posting, and calculating machine operator	344
Telephone operator	348
Communications equipment operator, n.e.c.	353
Electronic repair/communication/industrial equipment	523
Data processing equipment repairer	525
Household appliance and power tool repairer	526
Telephone line installer and repairer	527
Telephone installer and repairer	529
Miscellaneous electrical and electronic equipment repairer	533
Electrician	575
Electrician apprentice	576
Electrical power installer and repairer	577
Numerical control machine operator	714

NOTE: n.e.c. is "not elsewhere classified."

APPENDIX B

Regressions on Personnel Flows

The tables in this appendix present the results of probit regressions on entering an IT occupation (Table B.1), selection of an initial term of five or six years (Table B.2), attrition (Table B.3), and reenlistment (Table B.4). The attrition and reenlistment regressions are for personnel with term lengths of three, four, five, or six years. Attrition is measured at two years of service. We defined reenlistment by the condition that the member is present in the data file 3 months before and 12 months after his expiration of term of service (ETS) date. The explanatory variables include the individual's AFQT category, education level, gender, race/ethnicity, and fiscal year. Term length indicators are included in the attrition and reenlistment regressions.

The upper part of Tables B.5–B.16 show the coefficients for members in non-IT occupations, and the lower part shows the difference between the coefficients for members in IT occupations versus those in non-IT occupations. Coefficients for IT occupations may be obtained by summing the non-IT coefficient and the coefficient for the difference between the IT and non-IT coefficients.

The reference group in the regressions is white males with high school education and AFQT I–II. In the attrition and reenlistment regressions, the reference term length is four years. Coefficients on fiscal year indicators and "AFQT unknown" are not reported.

The PERSTEMPO data file is used in the regressions. It is a longitudinal, microdata file of active duty personnel maintained by the Defense Manpower Data Center (see Hosek and Totten, 1998 and 2002, for further description).

Table B.1
Probit Regressions on Entering an IT Occupation Versus a Non-IT Occupation: Army

Variable	Coefficient	Std. Error	Probability > Chi Sq
Intercept	–.4940	.0070	<.0001
AFQT IIIA	–.3403	.0053	<.0001
AFQT IIIB	–.7262	.0057	<.0001
AFQT IV	–.9694	.0194	<.0001
Non-HSG	.0184	.0089	.0378
GED	–.0890	.0100	<.0001
Some college	.1004	.0130	<.0001
Female	–.1115	.0057	<.0001
Black	.0228	.0055	<.0001
Hispanic	–.0007	.0076	.9245
Number of observations	459,671		
Log likelihood	–222,729		

Table B.2
Probit Regressions on Entering an IT Occupation Versus a Non-IT Occupation: Navy

Variable	Coefficient	Std. Error	Probability > Chi Sq
Intercept	–.7881	.0083	<.0001
AFQT IIIA	–.2584	.0062	<.0001
AFQT IIIB	–.6288	.0064	<.0001
AFQT IV	–.5209	.0476	<.0001
Non-HSG	–.0052	.0156	.7372
GED	.0138	.0098	.1558
Some college	–.9123	.0253	<.0001
Female	–.0943	.0068	<.0001
Black	.0284	.0067	<.0001
Hispanic	–.0575	.0081	<.0001
Number of observations	364,803		
Log likelihood	–170,693		

Table B.3
Probit Regressions on Entering an IT Occupation Versus a Non-IT Occupation: Marine Corps

Variable	Coefficient	Std. Error	Probability > Chi Sq
Intercept	–.7816	.0105	<.0001
AFQT IIIA	–.4750	.0077	<.0001
AFQT IIIB	–.8171	.0081	<.0001
AFQT IV	–1.0274	.0482	<.0001
Non-HSG	–.2124	.0712	.0028
GED	–.1067	.0158	<.0001
Some college	–.0456	.0322	.1568
Female	.1044	.0124	<.0001
Black	.2498	.0094	<.0001
Hispanic	.0532	.0098	<.0001
Number of observations	246,081		
Log likelihood	–104,168		

Table B.4
Probit Regressions on Entering an IT Occupation Versus a Non-IT Occupation: Air Force

Variable	Coefficient	Std. Error	Probability > Chi Sq
Intercept	–.3997	.0094	<.0001
AFQT IIIA	–.6442	.0069	<.0001
AFQT IIIB	–.9233	.0086	<.0001
AFQT IV	–1.1250	.0889	<.0001
Non-HSG	–.3487	.1241	.0050
GED	–.2764	.0285	<.0001
Some college	.0875	.0085	<.0001
Female	.2873	.0065	<.0001
Black	.1730	.0079	<.0001
Hispanic	.1375	.0123	<.0001
Number of observations	241,364		
Log likelihood	–130,216		

Table B.5
Probit Regressions on Selecting an Initial Term of Five or Six Years: Army

Variable	Coefficient	Std. Error	Probability > Chi Sq
Non-IT			
Intercept	–.7885	.0081	<.0001
AFQT IIIA	–.1586	.0069	<.0001
AFQT IIIB	–.5953	.0076	<.0001
AFQT IV	–.9162	.0283	<.0001
Non-HSG	–.0399	.0113	.0004
GED	–.2945	.0141	<.0001
Some college	.3302	.0165	<.0001
Female	.1444	.0071	<.0001
Black	–.2519	.0076	<.0001
Hispanic	–.1124	.0099	<.0001
IT versus non-IT			
IIntercept	.2289	.0116	<.0001
IAFQT I-II	–.0890	.0164	<.0001
IAFQT IIIA	–.2439	.0186	<.0001
IAFQT IIIB	–.1991	.0219	<.0001
IAFQT IV	–.2554	.0946	.0069
INon-HSG	.1321	.0197	<.0001
IGED	–.0894	.0295	.0024
ISome college	.0547	.0289	.0584
IFemale	.0904	.0141	<.0001
IBlack	.2980	.0147	<.0001
IHispanic	.1899	.0203	<.0001
Number of observations	459,671		
Log likelihood	–165,011		

NOTE: "I" at the beginning of a variable name indicates that the variable interacts with the indicator variable for IT occupations. The coefficients on the "I" variables equal the difference between the IT and the non-IT effects. For instance, the non-IT intercept is 0.7885, the difference between the IT intercept and the non-IT intercept is 0.2289, and therefore the IT intercept equals 0.7885 + 0.2289.

Table B.6
Probit Regressions on Selecting an Initial Term of Five or Six Years: Navy

Variable	Coefficient	Std. Error	Probability > Chi Sq
Non-IT			
Intercept	–2.9106	.0543	<.0001
AFQT IIIA	–.3938	.0100	<.0001
AFQT IIIB	–.6865	.0104	<.0001
AFQT IV	–.9547	.1063	<.0001
Non-HSG	–.4777	.0343	<.0001
GED	–.1624	.0173	<.0001
Some college	–.0067	.0231	.7700
Female	.1032	.0100	<.0001
Black	–.1224	.0113	<.0001
Hispanic	–.0737	.0131	<.0001
IT versus non-IT			
IIntercept	–.3420	.0195	<.0001
IAFQT I-II	.3060	.0268	<.0001
IAFQT IIIA	.2144	.0316	<.0001
IAFQT IIIB	–.0348	.0369	.3453
IAFQT IV	.1805	.2889	.5322
INon-HSG	.0780	.0699	.2645
IGED	.1147	.0360	.0015
ISome college	.1725	.0908	.0576
IFemale	–.2070	.0261	<.0001
IBlack	.0680	.0271	.0123
IHispanic	.0905	.0305	.0030
Number of observations	364,803		
Log likelihood	–78,211		

NOTE: See note for Table B.5.

Table B.7
Probit Regressions on Selecting an Initial Term of Five or Six Years: Marine Corps

Variable	Coefficient	Std. Error	Probability > Chi Sq
Non-IT			
Intercept	–.5878	.0106	<.0001
AFQT IIIA	–.3558	.0095	<.0001
AFQT IIIB	–.8891	.0109	<.0001
AFQT IV	–1.3302	.0795	<.0001
Non-HSG	–.1688	.0824	.0406
GED	–.1108	.0197	<.0001
Some college	–.1318	.0439	.0027
Female	–.1545	.0178	<.0001
Black	–.2900	.0149	<.0001
Hispanic	–.1535	.0130	<.0001

Table B.7—continued

Variable	Coefficient	Std. Error	Probability > Chi Sq
IT versus non-IT			
IIntercept	–.7369	.0168	<.0001
IAFQT I-II	1.8886	.0240	<.0001
IAFQT IIIA	1.3890	.0266	<.0001
IAFQT IIIB	.8311	.0379	<.0001
IAFQT IV	1.7932	.1962	<.0001
INon-HSG	–.6654	.2098	.0015
IGED	–.3678	.0453	<.0001
ISome college	.2208	.0773	.0043
IFemale	–.0445	.0331	.1782
IBlack	.0928	.0276	.0008
IHispanic	.1742	.0266	<.0001
Number of observations	246,081		
Log likelihood	–81,893		

NOTE: See note for Table B.5.

Table B.8
Probit Regressions on Selecting an Initial Term of Five or Six Years: Air Force

Variable	Coefficient	Std. Error	Probability > Chi Sq
Non-IT			
Intercept	.0640	.0102	<.0001
AFQT IIIB	–.2784	.0112	<.0001
AFQT IV	–1.2757	.1345	<.0001
AFQT IIIA	–.1768	.0102	<.0001
Non-HSG	–.7106	.3059	.0202
GED	.1503	.0316	<.0001
Some college	–.3248	.0165	<.0001
Female	–.4235	.0107	<.0001
Black	–.1465	.0119	<.0001
Hispanic	–.1191	.0185	<.0001
IT versus non-IT			
IIntercept	–.4367	.0138	<.0001
IAFQT I-II	–.0242	.0420	.5649
IAFQT IIIA	1.2699	.4577	.0055
IAFQT IIIB	.5765	.0270	<.0001
IAFQT IV	.7937	.0225	<.0001
INon-HSG	–3.8362	435.4150	.9930
IGED	–.3922	.0704	<.0001
ISome college	.0499	.0258	.053
IFemale	.2579	.0187	<.0001
IBlack	–.0221	.0229	.3358
IHispanic	.0245	.0343	.4760
Number of observations	241,364		
Log likelihood	–80,435		

NOTE: See note for Table B.5.

Table B.9
Probit Regressions on Attrition: Army

Variable	Coefficient	Std. Error	Probability > Chi Sq
Non-IT			
Intercept	–.9149	.0121	<.0001
AFQT IIIA	.1009	.0093	<.0001
AFQT IIIB	.1127	.0093	<.0001
AFQT IV	.0390	.0229	.0884
Non-HSG	.0642	.0253	.0111
GED	.2738	.0170	<.0001
Some college	–.1179	.0214	<.0001
Female	.2789	.0085	<.0001
Black	–.1376	.0083	<.0001
Hispanic	–.2569	.0125	<.0001
3-yr. term	–.0180	.0071	.0108
5-yr. term	.0381	.0148	.0102
6-yr. term	–.1188	.0247	<.0001
IT versus non-IT			
IIntercept	.0287	.0178	.1080
IAFQT I–II	–.0875	.0249	.0004
IAFQT IIIA	–.0667	.0270	.0137
IAFQT IIIB	–.0776	.0277	.0052
IAFQT IV	–.1248	.0856	.1445
INon-HSG	–.0990	.0979	.3121
IGED	.0195	.0389	.6155
ISome college	–.1743	.0425	<.0001
IFemale	.0826	.0199	<.0001
IBlack	.0293	.0199	.1414
IHispanic	.0378	.0306	.2163
Number of observations	248,123		
Log likelihood	–108,301		

NOTE: See note for Table B.5.

Table B.10
Probit Regressions on Attrition: Navy

Variable	Coefficient	Std. Error	Probability > Chi Sq
Non-IT			
Intercept	–.9622	.0161	<.0001
AFQT IIIA	.0372	.0105	.0004
AFQT IIIB	.0820	.0100	<.0001
AFQT IV	.0956	.0621	.1239
Non-HSG	.3847	.0278	<.0001
GED	.3500	.0153	<.0001
Some college	–.1416	.0268	<.0001
Female	–.0048	.0102	.6373
Black	–.0252	.0101	.0124
Hispanic	–.1681	.0127	<.0001
3-yr. term	.0198	.0097	.0408
5-yr. term	–.1526	.0170	<.0001
6-yr. term	–.0466	.0228	.0407

Table B.10—continued

Variable	Coefficient	Std. Error	Probability > Chi Sq
IT versus non-IT			
IIntercept	–.2136	.0203	<.0001
IAFQT I–II	–.0073	.0297	.8050
IAFQT IIIA	.0564	.0316	.0746
IAFQT IIIB	.0573	.0298	.0543
IAFQT IV	.0834	.1603	.6027
INon-HSG	–.0315	.0585	.5901
IGED	.0161	.0341	.6377
ISome college	.2086	.0967	.0310
IFemale	.1416	.0248	<.0001
IBlack	.0015	.0244	.9525
IHispanic	–.0129	.0314	.6799
Number of observations	195,069		
Log likelihood	–85,227		

NOTE: See note for Table B.5.

Table B.11
Probit Regressions on Attrition: Marine Corps

Variable	Coefficient	Std. Error	Probability > Chi Sq
Non-IT			
Intercept	–1.0295	.0225	<.0001
AFQT IIIA	.0346	.0126	.0060
AFQT IIIB	.0831	.0120	<.0001
AFQT IV	.0304	.0646	.6385
Non-HSG	.4186	.1009	<.0001
GED	.3372	.0202	<.0001
Some college	.0858	.0481	.0744
Female	.2655	.0191	<.0001
Black	–.0092	.0139	.5092
Hispanic	–.2563	.0154	<.0001
3-yr. term	.5207	.0675	<.0001
5-yr. term	.0770	.0212	.0003
6-yr. term	–.0228	.0438	.6030
IT versus non-IT			
IIntercept	.1347	.0320	<.0001
IAFQT I–II	–.9103	.0499	<.0001
IAFQT IIIA	–.6952	.0541	<.0001
IAFQT IIIB	–.5898	.0551	<.0001
IAFQT IV	–.3064	.2501	.2204
INon-HSG	–.1915	.3749	.6096
IGED	–.0172	.0688	.8029
ISome college	.6462	.1096	<.0001
IFemale	.1409	.0489	.0039
IBlack	.1446	.0412	.0004
IHispanic	.0380	.0552	.4919
Number of observations.	134,222		
Log likelihood	–50,332		

NOTE: See note for Table B.5.

Table B.12
Probit Regressions on Attrition: Air Force

Variable	Coefficient	Std. Error	Probability > Chi Sq
Non-IT			
Intercept	−1.1506	.0230	<.0001
AFQT IIIA	.0363	.0128	.0046
AFQT IIIB	.0495	.0147	.0007
AFQT IV	.1730	.1052	.1000
Non-HSG	.3113	.1663	.0613
GED	.3012	.0532	<.0001
Some college	−.2842	.0171	<.0001
Female	.0745	.0126	<.0001
Black	.0426	.0147	.0038
Hispanic	−.1147	.0247	<.0001
3-yr. term	−.0555	.4042	.8908
5-yr. term	.3738	.1361	.0060
6-yr. term	.1009	.0517	.0512
IT versus non-IT			
IIntercept	.0391	.0238	.1009
IAFQT I–II	−.3055	.0582	<.0001
IAFQT IIIA	−.7400	.4899	.1309
IAFQT IIIB	−.4703	.0470	<.0001
IAFQT IV	−.5602	.0411	<.0001
INon-HSG	.3233	.3874	.4039
IGED	.0363	.1632	.8240
ISome college	.0426	.0373	.2531
IFemale	.0994	.0279	.0004
IBlack	.0144	.0340	.6715
IHispanic	−.0301	.0601	.6168
Number of observations	130,857		
Log likelihood	−40,918		

NOTE: See note for Table B.5.

Table B.13
Probit Regressions on First-Term Reenlistment: Army

Variable	Coefficient	Std. Error	Probability > Chi Sq
Non-IT			
Intercept	−.0925	.0109	<.0001
AFQT IIIA	.0709	.0099	<.0001
AFQT IIIB	.0902	.0101	<.0001
AFQT IV	.1474	.0229	<.0001
Non-HSG	−.0099	.0363	.7847
GED	.1922	.0209	<.0001
Some college	−.0326	.0212	.1252
Female	.0812	.0105	<.0001
Black	.3772	.0093	<.0001
Hispanic	.1554	.0129	<.0001
3-yr. term	−.1353	.0077	<.0001
5-yr. term	−.0598	.0172	.0005
6-yr. term	.0348	.0255	.1722

Table B.13—continued

Variable	Coefficient	Std. Error	Probability > Chi Sq
IT versus Non-IT			
IIntercept	.0188	.0193	.3311
IAFQT I–II	–.1075	.0266	<.0001
IAFQT IIIA	–.1037	.0292	.0004
IAFQT IIIB	–.1150	.0297	.0001
IAFQT IV	.0157	.0831	.8506
INon-HSG	.1807	.1113	.1044
IGED	–.0102	.0471	.8291
ISome college	–.1601	.0392	<.0001
IFemale	–.0298	.0246	.2254
IBlack	–.0137	.0216	.5250
IHispanic	.0368	.0305	.2271
Number of observations	142,874		
Log likelihood	–96,046		

NOTE: See note for Table B.5.

Table B.14
Probit Regressions on First-Term Reenlistment: Navy

Variable	Coefficient	Std. Error	Probability > Chi Sq
Non-IT			
Intercept	.3830	.0117	<.0001
AFQT IIIA	–.2320	.0113	<.0001
AFQT IIIB	–.2745	.0111	<.0001
AFQT IV	–.0148	.0760	.8454
Non-HSG	.0014	.0386	.9709
GED	.0294	.0211	.1646
Some college	–.0076	.0270	.7793
Female	.0361	.0116	.0018
Black	.3651	.0117	<.0001
Hispanic	.1112	.0138	<.0001
3-yr. term	–.3427	.0107	<.0001
5-yr. term	–.0034	.0173	.8436
6-yr. term	–.1157	.0245	<.0001
IT versus non-IT			
IIntercept	–.1668	.0186	<.0001
IAFQT I–II	.1093	.0282	.0001
IAFQT IIIA	.0875	.0304	.0040
IAFQT IIIB	.0516	.0288	.0729
IAFQT IV	.2211	.1668	.1850
INon-HSG	.1057	.0715	.1391
IGED	.0434	.0416	.2957
ISome college	–.1577	.0943	.0945
IFemale	–.0007	.0262	.9791
IBlack	.0376	.0251	.1337
IHispanic	–.0337	.0298	.2576
Number of observations	115,869		
Log likelihood	–76,623		

NOTE: See note for Table B.5.

Table B.15
Probit Regressions on First-Term Reenlistment: Marine Corps

Variable	Coefficient	Std. Error	Probability > Chi Sq
Non-IT			
Intercept	–.7111	.0147	<.0001
AFQT IIIA	–.0268	.0135	.0467
AFQT IIIB	–.0701	.0130	<.0001
AFQT IV	–.0032	.0760	.9663
Non-HSG	.2260	.1400	.1065
GED	.0417	.0278	.1340
Some college	–.0536	.0585	.3594
Female	.1629	.0242	<.0001
Black	.4535	.0154	<.0001
Hispanic	.2223	.0158	<.0001
3-yr. term	.2949	.1043	.0047
5-yr. term	.1876	.0225	<.0001
6-yr. term	.2566	.0330	<.0001
IT versus non-IT			
IIntercept	–.0380	.0264	.1492
IAFQT I–II	.1032	.0388	.0079
IAFQT IIIA	.1253	.0439	.0043
IAFQT IIIB	.0929	.0461	.0438
IAFQT IV	.0426	.2466	.8629
INon-HSG	–.1445	.3940	.7138
IGED	.0248	.0697	.7223
ISome college	–.3444	.1391	.0133
IFemale	–.0286	.0513	.5768
IBlack	–.0886	.0371	.0168
IHispanic	–.0310	.0406	.4453
Number of observations	86,683		
Log likelihood	–45,371		

NOTE: See note for Table B.5.

Table B.16
Probit Regressions on First-Term Reenlistment: Air Force

Variable	Coefficient	Std. Error	Probability > Chi Sq
Non-IT			
Intercept	.1164	.0132	<.0001
AFQT IIIA	.0358	.0118	.0023
AFQT IIIB	.1035	.0138	<.0001
AFQT IV	.0322	.1098	.7692
Non-HSG	.2966	.1973	.1326
GED	.2054	.0617	.0009
Some college	–.0649	.0144	<.0001
Female	.0663	.0124	<.0001
Black	.3464	.0150	<.0001
Hispanic	.0895	.0223	<.0001
3-yr. term	.0393	.6293	.9502
5-yr. term	–.0884	.1345	.5113
6-yr. term	–.0078	.0461	.8665

Table B.16—continued

Variable	Coefficient	Std. Error	Probability > Chi Sq
IT versus non-IT			
IIntercept	–.0488	.0166	.0033
IAFQT I–II	.0614	.0288	.0330
IAFQT IIIA	.1422	.0340	<.0001
IAFQT IIIB	.2024	.0451	<.0001
IAFQT IV	.7758	.4313	.0721
INon-HSG	–.3967	.3894	.3083
IGED	–.0932	.1441	.5178
ISome college	–.0777	.0254	.0022
IFemale	.0142	.0226	.5293
IBlack	–.0324	.0285	.2550
IHispanic	–.0206	.0430	.6319
Number of observations	87,733		
Log likelihood	–59,062		

NOTE: See note for Table B.5.

APPENDIX C

Military/Civilian Pay Comparisons for Men and Women with More Than Four Years of College

Recognizing that many officers have more than four years of college, in this appendix we compare military compensation with civilian wages for officers and workers with more than four years of college. This supplements the comparison reported in Chapter Five, which looks at individuals with four or more years of college. The comparisons for men appear in Figure C.1. and those for women are in Figure C.2. As in the text, military compensation is measured in terms of regular military compensation, and civilian earnings are self-reports of usual earnings from the Current Population Survey.

For men in non-IT occupations, we find that officer RMC is approximately equal to the 70th percentile of civilian wages for men with more than four years of college over years of service 1–17. RMC is just below the 80th percentile in years 18–20. For men in IT-related or IT-core occupations, RMC is low the first few years of service, around the 30th percentile of civilian wages. In years 5–11, RMC is at the 60th percentile, in years 12–17 it is at the 70th percentile, and in years 18–20 it is somewhat below the 80th percentile.

For women in non-IT occupations, we find that officer RMC starts at the 70th percentile of civilian wages for women with more than four years of college. It exceeds the 80th percentile by year of service 5 and exceeds the 90th percentile at year 17. For women in IT-related and IT-core occupations, RMC begins at the 40th percentile of civilian wages, equals the 70th percentile in years 5–11, equals the 80th percentile in years 12–17, and reaches nearly the 90th percentile in years 18–20.

Figure C.1
Weekly Civilian Wage Percentiles for Men with More Than Four Years of College and Regular Military Compensation for Officers, by Service and IT Group, FY 2002

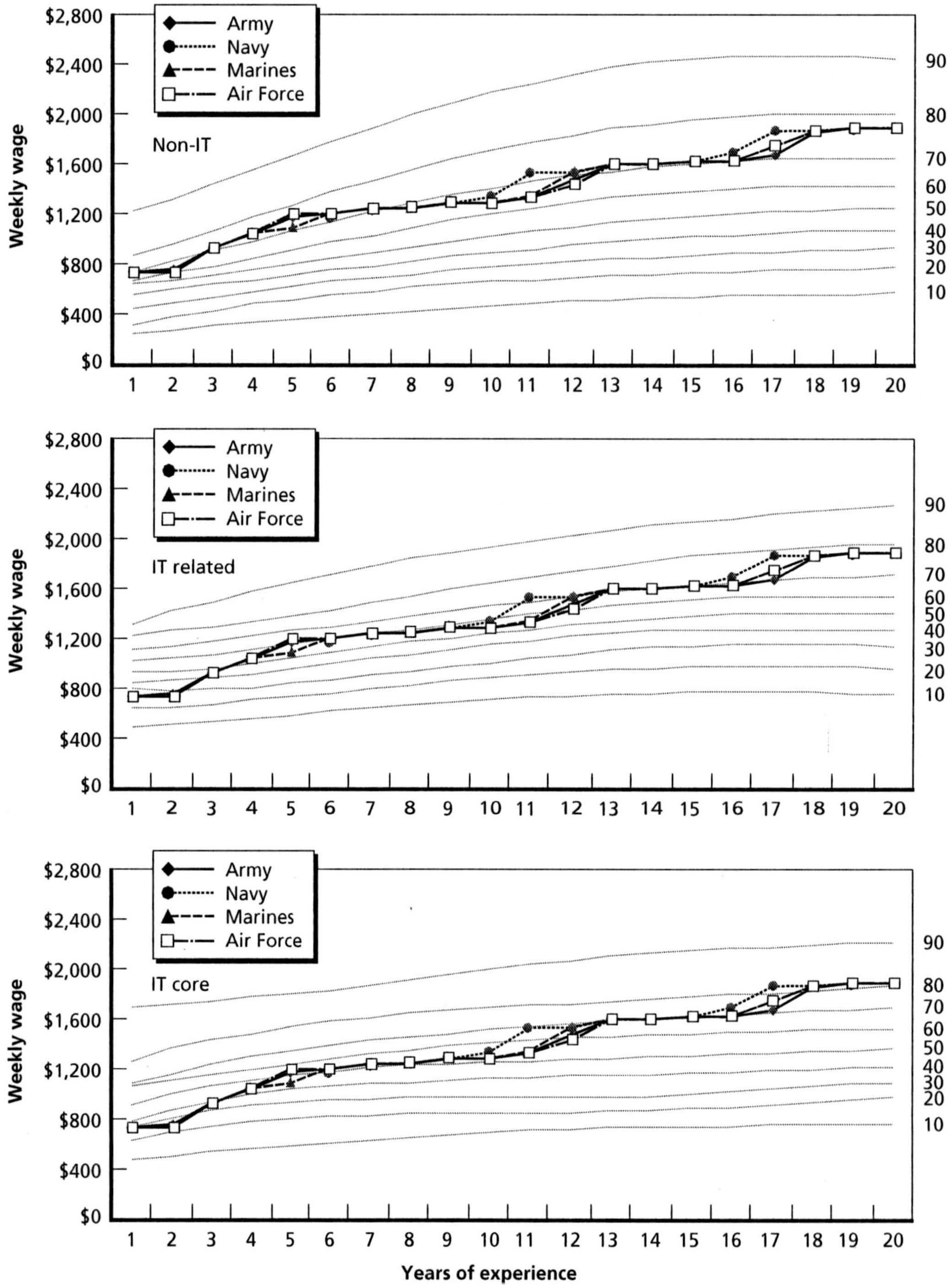

RAND *MG108-C.1*

Figure C.2
Weekly Civilian Wage Percentiles for Women with More Than Four Years of College and Regular Military Compensation for Officers, by Service and IT Group, FY 2002

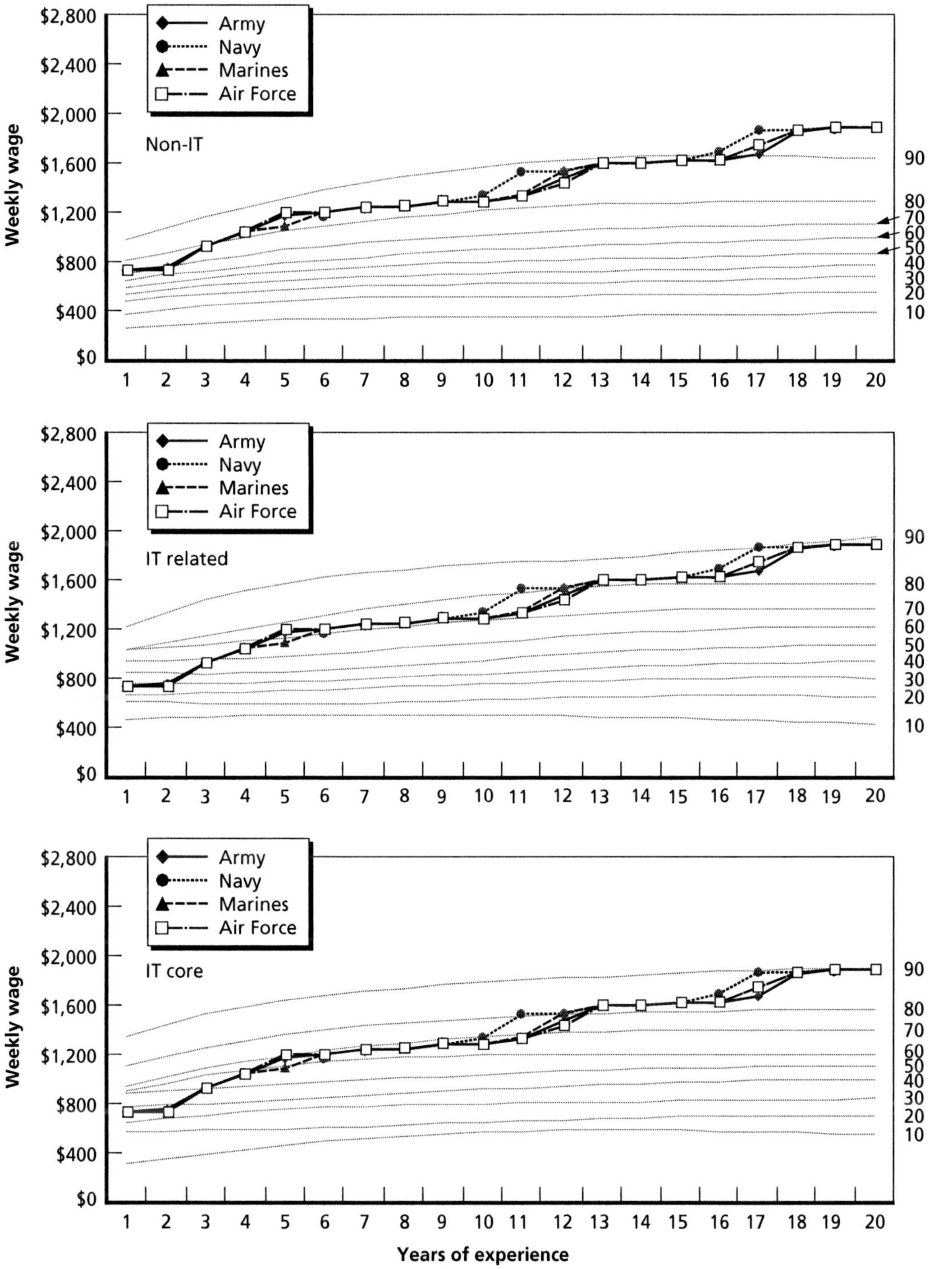

RAND *MG108-C.2*

APPENDIX D

Dynamic Retention Model with Enlistment

This appendix describes our model and the functions on which it is based. The model includes not only the wage incentives involved in the choice to enlist, but also the role of personnel preferences for military service. As stated above, our model is based on the dynamic retention model of Gotz and McCall (1984), which is a dynamic programming model of the decision to continue in military service. We believe that our extended model offers more reasonable predictions of junior retention and provides a natural way of distinguishing between retention during a contract and reenlistment at the end of the contract.

Model Structure

We assume that a person can enter the military for the first time in any year, and a person who leaves the military cannot reenter it. Let t index years of work life and let y index years of military service. In each year a person is either in the civilian world and has not yet entered the military (ante military, or "AM"), in the military ("M"), or out of the military and back in the civilian world (post military, or "PM"). The value of the ante-military program equals the current civilian wage plus the discounted value of the expected value of the optimal program in the next period, either remaining a civilian or entering the military. The value of the military program equals current military pay, plus one's preference for military service, plus the discounted value of the optimal program in the next period, either remaining in the military or leaving. The value of the post-military program equals the stream of civilian wages earned after leaving the military, plus military retirement benefits if any.

$$V^{AM}(t, y=0, \gamma) = W^{c}(t, y=0) + \beta E_t V^{1}(t+1, y=0, \gamma).$$

$$V^{M}(t, y, \gamma) = \gamma + W^{m}(y) + \beta E_t V^{2}(t+1, y+1, \gamma).$$

$$V^{PM}(t, y) = W^{c}(t, y) + \sum_{\tau=t+1}^{T} \beta^{\tau-t} W^{c}(\tau, y) + R(\beta, y).$$

Here, the person's taste for military service is γ. The personal discount rate is β, and E_t takes the expectation given the information at time t. The civilian wage W^c in general depends on effective years of labor force experience, which is some combination of work in the civilian sector and military service, discussed below. The military wage W^m depends only on years of military service. (We ignore military rank and promotion probabilities, although these can be treated as in Gotz and McCall, 1984.) The term $R(\beta, y)$ is the discounted value of military retirement benefits for a member with y years of service.

The functions V^1 and V^2 specify that the person optimizes when considering whether to enter the military or to remain in the military.

$$V^1(t, y, \gamma) = \max(V^{AM}(t, y = 0, \gamma) + \varepsilon_t^{AM}, V^M(t, y = 0, \gamma) + \varepsilon_t^M).$$

$$V^2(t, y, \gamma) = \max(V^M(t, y, \gamma) + \varepsilon_t^{AM}, V^{PM}(t, y) + \varepsilon_t^{PM}).$$

These decisions are affected by random disturbances realized at the beginning of the period, before any decision is made for that period. We assume the disturbances are normally distributed with zero mean and constant variance, and the variance of the civilian disturbance is the same regardless of whether it occurs before or after military service.

There are terminal points to civilian and military careers. The end of work life occurs at T, and the mandatory end of military service occurs at Y ($T > Y$). Hence

$$V^{AM}(T + 1, y = 0, \gamma) = 0.$$

$$V^M(t, Y + 1, \gamma) = 0.$$

$$V^{PM}(T + 1, y, \gamma) = 0.$$

Enlistment

In our model, a person enters the military at the beginning of period t if

$$V^M(t, y = 0, \gamma) + \varepsilon_t^M > V^{AM}(t, y = 0, \gamma) + \varepsilon_t^{AM}.$$

We define the propensity to join the military as

$$\begin{aligned} J_t^* &= (V^M(t, y = 0, \gamma) - V^{AM}(t, y = 0, \gamma)) + (\varepsilon_t^M - \varepsilon_t^{AM}) \\ &= a_t(\gamma) + \varepsilon_t, \end{aligned}$$

where $a_t(\gamma) = V^M(t, y = 0, \gamma) - V^{AM}(t, y = 0, \gamma)$ and $\varepsilon_t = \varepsilon_t^M - \varepsilon_t^{AM}$. The join and non-join indicators are

$$\begin{aligned} J_t &= 1 \quad \textit{if } J_t^* \geq 0 \\ &= 0 \quad \textit{if } J_t^* < 0. \end{aligned}$$

Since the disturbances are normal, their differences are normal. So the probability a person with taste γ joins at period t is

$$\Pr(J_t = 1;\gamma) = F(\frac{a_t(\gamma)}{\sigma}),$$

where $F(x)$ is the normal cumulative distribution function.

Solving for $E_{t-1}(V_t^1)$, we find that the expected value in $t-1$ of the maximum of joining or not joining equals the probability of joining times the value of joining plus the probability of not joining times the expected value of civilian earnings given that they exceed the threshold of not joining:

$$E_{t-1}(V_t^1) = F(\frac{a_t(\gamma)}{\sigma})V_t^M + (1 - F(\frac{a_t(\gamma)}{\sigma}))\, V_t^{AM} + \sigma f(\frac{a_t(\gamma)}{\sigma}),$$

where $f(x)$ is the normal probability density function.

Assuming that the preference for serving in the military is distributed as $g(\gamma)$ in a population cohort, then the fraction of the initial cohort joining at the beginning of the first year of work life is

$$\int_{-\infty}^{\infty} \Pr(J_0=1;\gamma)\, g(\gamma)\, d\gamma.$$

At the beginning of the second year it is

$$\int_{-\infty}^{\infty} \Pr(J_0=0;\gamma)\Pr(J_1=1;\gamma)g(\gamma)\,d\gamma,$$

and at the beginning of year t it is

$$\int_{-\infty}^{\infty} \prod_{\tau=0}^{t-2} \Pr(J_\tau=0;\gamma)\Pr(J_{t-1}=1;\gamma)g(\gamma)\,d\gamma.$$

Expressions like these can be used to construct the distribution of γ for those entering the military. In any given period, the military enlists people of different ages who therefore come from different labor-market entrant cohorts. This implies that the distribution of γ in an entering cohort of recruits is a mixture of the γ distributions of recruits from the various labor-market cohorts. If we assume the recruitment process is in a steady state and labor-market cohorts are of equal size, the γ distribution of those joining in a given period equals the sum of the joint probability of γ and joining in period one, plus the joint probability of γ and joining in period two, allowing for the γ distribution being depleted of the first-period joiners, and so forth. Using Bayes' theorem, this can be written:

$$\Pr(\gamma \mid Join) = \Pr(J_0 = 1 \mid \gamma) g(\gamma) + \Pr(J_1 = 1 \mid \gamma) \frac{\Pr(J_0 = 0 \mid \gamma) g(\gamma)}{\int \Pr(J_0 = 0 \mid \gamma) g(\gamma) d\gamma}$$
$$+ \Pr(J_2 = 1 \mid \gamma) \frac{\Pr(J_1 = 0 \mid \gamma) \Pr(J_0 = 0 \mid \gamma) g(\gamma)}{\int \Pr(J_1 = 0 \mid \gamma) \Pr(J_0 = 0 \mid \gamma) g(\gamma) d\gamma} + \ldots.$$

We refer to the distribution of γ among new recruits as $gm(\gamma)$, i.e.,

$$\Pr(\gamma \mid Join) \equiv gm(\gamma),$$

whereas the distribution of γ in the population cohort is $g(\gamma)$. Because we assume a steady state, $gm(\gamma)$ is constant over time as is $g(\gamma)$. However, if we follow a given cohort of youth from period to period, the distribution of γ among youth who have not (yet) enlisted will evolve, as those with a low preference for military service stay out of the military, while those with a high preference enter the military. Similarly, for a given cohort of new recruits, the distribution $gm(\gamma)$ will evolve over years of service, as those with a low preference for military service separate. We show how $gm(\gamma)$ evolves below by computing the posterior distribution of γ conditional on retention to year of service y.

Retention

Our model can also simulate the retention of enlisted members at the end of their first term. A member chooses to stay in the military at the beginning of t if $V^M(t, y, \gamma) + \varepsilon_t^M > V^{PM}(t, y) + \varepsilon_t^{PM}$. The decision depends on the year of service and the year of work life. Military pay increases with years of service, and civilian wage increases with years of experience, including years in the military. A member who served four years and worked four years before entering service will have a different civilian wage than a member who served eight years and had no prior civilian work experience. In addition, the member who entered the military immediately probably had a higher preference for military service than the member who first worked for four years.

Define the propensity to stay in the military as

$$S_{ty}^* = (V^M(t, y, \gamma) - V^{PM}(t, y,)) + (\varepsilon_t^M - \varepsilon_t^{PM})$$
$$= b_{ty}(\gamma) + \varepsilon_t.$$

where $b_{ty}(\gamma) = V^M(t, y, \gamma) - V^{PM}(t, y,)$ and $\varepsilon_t = (\varepsilon_t^M - \varepsilon_t^{PM})$. The stay and leave indicators are:

$$S_{ty} = 1 \; if \; S_{ty}^* \geq 0$$
$$= 0 \; if \; S_{ty}^* < 0.$$

Since the disturbances are normal, their difference is normal. So the probability a member with preference γ stays in the military is

$$\Pr(S_{ty} = 1; \gamma) = F(\frac{b_{ty}(\gamma)}{\sigma}).$$

Solving for $E_{t-1}(V_t^2)$, we find that the expected value of the maximum of staying or leaving equals the probability of staying times the value of staying, plus the probability of leaving times the expected value of civilian earnings given that they exceed the threshold for staying.

$$E_{t-1}(V_t^2) = F(\frac{b_{ty}(\gamma)}{\sigma})V_t^M + (1 - F(\frac{b_{ty}(\gamma)}{\sigma}))\, V_t^{PM} + \sigma f(\frac{b_{ty}(\gamma)}{\sigma}).$$

Recalling that γ is distributed as $gm(\gamma)$ among recruits, the fraction of recruits staying in service for a second year is

$$\int_{-\infty}^{\infty} \Pr(S_0 = 1; \gamma) \Pr(S_1 = 1; \gamma)\, gm(\gamma)\, d\gamma.$$

However, $\Pr(S_0 = 1; \gamma) = 1$; because at the outset of the first year of service, each recruit in effect has decided to stay or else he or she would not have entered service in the first place. Choosing to enter is equivalent to choosing to stay at the beginning of the first year of service. The fraction of recruits staying for t years is

$$\int_{-\infty}^{\infty} \prod_{\tau=0}^{t-1} \Pr(S_\tau = 1; \gamma)\, gm(\gamma)\, d\gamma,$$

which we use to compute the retention profile of a cohort of new members. Finally, the year-to-year retention rate for year t relative to year $t-1$ is

$$\left(\int_{-\infty}^{\infty} \prod_{\tau=0}^{t-1} \Pr(S_\tau = 1; \gamma)\, gm(\gamma)\, d\gamma \right) \Big/ \left(\int_{-\infty}^{\infty} \prod_{\tau=0}^{t-2} \Pr(S_\tau = 1; \gamma)\, gm(\gamma)\, d\gamma \right).$$

This is also commonly referred to as the year-to-year continuation rate.

Adding Breaching Costs

As we discussed in Chapter Six, breaching costs apply if the member leaves in a period prior to the end of the contract. We included these costs in our model to look more closely at the function the enlistment contract plays in the military's attrition rate. The costs are represented by the term $k(y)$:

$$V^{PM}(t, y) = W^c(t, y) - k(y) + \sum_{\tau=t+1}^{T} \beta^{\tau-t} W^c(\tau, y) + R(\beta, y).$$

In this specification, the cost $k(y)$ is borne only at period t, the first period upon leaving, and not in future periods. Thus, there is no cost subtracted from civilian wages in future periods.

Model Calibration Without and With Breaching Costs

For each of the services, the model was calibrated to year-to-year retention rates for recruits with an initial obligation of four years by minimizing the sum of squared residuals, subject to the constraint that the probability of joining was 0.08. The calibration resulted in fitted parameter values for the distribution of tastes $g(\gamma)$; we assumed the taste distribution was an extreme value distribution, with mode α and scale parameter δ. In addition, the calibration also resulted in a value for σ^2, the variance of the shock distribution. In doing the calibration, we held the discount parameter fixed at $\beta = 0.88$.

We calibrated the model both with and without breaching costs and found that the fit of the model was considerably improved by including these costs. Breaching costs were constrained to be greater than or equal to zero; costs in year four (at the end of the initial obligation) were assumed to be zero. Figure D.1 shows the fit of the Army model without and with breaching costs. As can be seen from the figure, the addition of breaching costs lowers the predicted rate of attrition in the initial years, and also lowers reenlistment to a realistic level. Figures D.2 and D.3 show similar results for the Air Force and Navy.

We used the model to produce a series of calculations that show the effect of shifting from the non-IT civilian wage line used in calibrating the model to a civilian wage that is dependent on military IT training and experience (the IT-transition wage line). The figures in Chapter Six show the effect of this shift on retention, the distribution of taste for military service among new entrants into military service, and the evolution of that distribution as years of service increase.

Figure D.1
Army Model Fit, Without Cost of Breach (left panel) and With Cost of Breach (right panel)

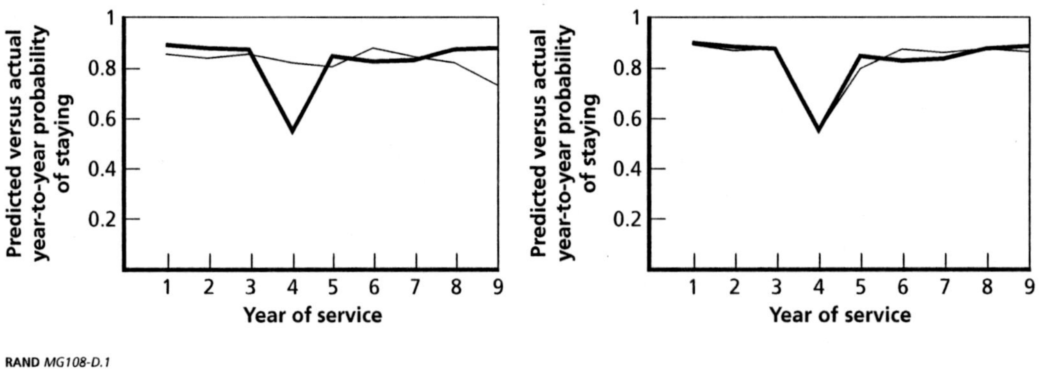

Figure D.2
Air Force Model Fit, Without Cost of Breach (left panel) and With Cost of Breach (right panel)

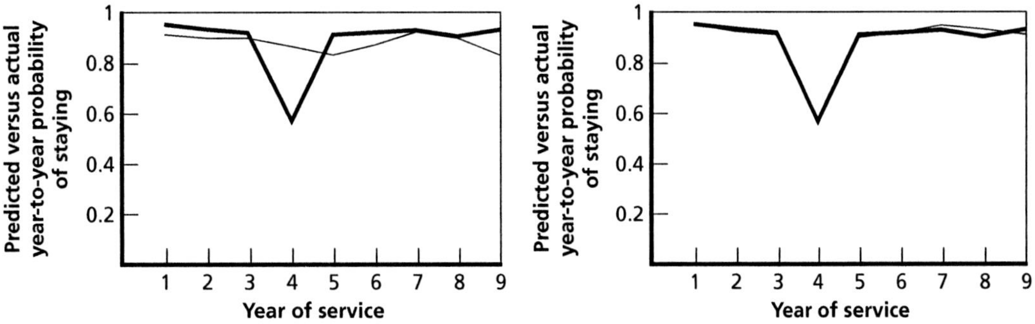

RAND *MG108-D.2*

Figure D.3
Navy Model Fit, Without Cost of Breach (left panel) and With Cost of Breach (right panel)

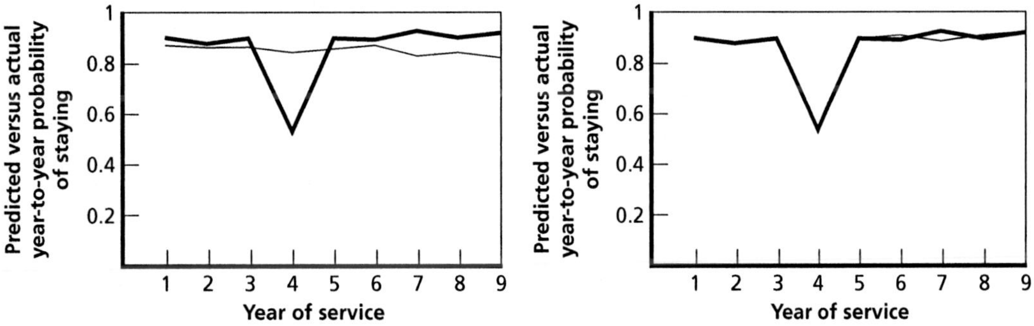

RAND *MG108-D.3*

Bibliography

Asch, Beth, C. Christine Fair, and M. Rebecca Kilburn, *An Assessment of Recent Proposals to Improve the Montgomery GI Bill*, Santa Monica, Calif.: RAND Corporation, DB-301-OSD/FRP, 2000.

Asch, Beth J., James R. Hosek, Jeremy Arkes, C. Christine Fair, Jennifer Sharp, and Mark Totten, *Military Recruiting and Retention After the Fiscal Year 2000 Military Pay Legislation*, Santa Monica, Calif.: RAND Corporation, MR-1532-OSD, 2002.

Asch, Beth J., James R. Hosek, and Craig W. Martin, *A Look at Cash Compensation for Active Duty Military Personnel*, Santa Monica, Calif.: RAND Corporation, MR-1492-OSD, 2002.

Asch, Beth, James R. Hosek, and John T. Warner, *An Analysis of Pay for Enlisted Personnel*, Santa Monica, Calif.: RAND Corporation, DB-344-OSD, 2001.

Asch, Beth, Richard Johnson, and John Warner, *Reforming the Military Retirement System*, Santa Monica, Calif.: RAND Corporation, MR-748-OSD, 1998.

Asch, Beth, and John T. Warner, *A Theory of Military Compensation and Personnel Policy*, Santa Monica, Calif.: RAND Corporation, MR-439-OSD, 1994.

Autor, David H., Frank Levy, and Richard J. Murnane, *The Skill Content of Recent Technological Change*, National Bureau of Economic Research, Working Paper 8337, June 2001, www.nber.org/papers/w8337, last accessed May 1, 2003.

Banda, Sara, "Bonus Program Gives Officers More Incentive to Stay," *Air Force Print News*, March 29, 2002, www.af.mil/news/, last accessed November 11, 2003.

Bonjour, Dorothe, Lynn Cherkas, Jonathan Haskel, Denise Hawkes, and Tim Spector, *Estimating Returns to Education Using a New Sample of UK Twins*, London: Center for the Economics of Education, London School of Economics and Political Science, April 2002.

Bresnahan, Timothy, *Computerization and Wage Dispersion: An Analytical Reinterpretation*, draft, August 1997, www.stanford.edu/~tbres/research.htm.

Bresnahan, Timothy, *The Mechanisms of Information Technology's Contribution to Economic Growth*, presentation at the Saint-Gobain Center for Economic Research Conference "What Do We Know About the Sources of Technical Change," undated, www.stanford.edu/~tbres/research/mechanisms_of_it_contribution.pdf, last accessed May 1, 2003.

Bresnahan, Timothy, and Manuel Trajtenberg, "General Purpose Technologies: Engines of Growth?" *Journal of Econometrics*, Vol. 65, No. 1, January 1995, pp. 83–108.

Cooke, Timothy W., and Aline Quester, "What Characterizes Successful Enlistees in the All-Volunteer Force: A Study of Male Recruits in the U.S. Navy," *Social Science Quarterly*, Vol. 72, 1992, pp. 238–252.

Daula, Thomas, and Robert Moffitt, "Estimating Dynamic Models of Quit Behavior: The Case of Military Re-enlistment," *Journal of Labor Economics*, Vol. 13, No. 3, July 1995, pp. 449–523.

Davis, Bob, and David Wessel, "Making It Simple: How Technology Will Make Life Better for Less Skilled Workers," *Army Times*, May 18, 1998, pp. 24–25.

Davis, Bob, and David Wessel, *Prosperity: The Coming Twenty-Year Boom and What It Means to You*, New York: Times Books, 1999.

Davis, Rep. Tom, "Transforming the IT and Acquisition Workforces: Using Market-Based Pay, Recruiting and Retention Strategies to Make the Federal Government an Employer of Choice for IT and Acquisition Employees," Opening Statement, Subcommittee on Technology and Procurement Policy Legislative Hearing, U.S. House of Representatives, October 4, 2001, http://web.archive.org/web/20021219000301/http://reform.house.gov/tapps/hearings/10-4-01/OPM.htm, last accessed December 2003.

Federal Acquisition Report, Vol. XVIII, No. 10, November 2001, pp. 1, 3.

Fernandez, J., "Soldier Quality and Job Performance in Team Tasks," *Social Science Quarterly*, Vol. 73, 1992, pp. 253–265.

Fernandez, Richard, Glenn A. Gotz, and Robert Bell, *The Dynamic Retention Model*, Santa Monica, Calif.: RAND Corporation, N-2141-MIL, 1985.

"Force Accounting and System Division: TRADOC Review of Manpower," www.tradoc.army.mil/dcsrm/trm.htm, last accessed August 19, 2003.

Forman, Mark, Office of Management and Budget, testimony before the House Subcommittee on Technology and Procurement Policy of the Committee on Government Reform, U.S. House of Representatives, 2001, http://web.archive.org/web/20030309115236/http://reform.house.gov/tapps/hearings/10-4-01/Forman.htm, last accessed December 2003.

Freeman, Peter, and William Aspray, *The Supply of Information Technology Workers in the United States*, Washington, D.C.: Computing Research Association, 1999.

Goldberg, Matthew, "A Survey of Enlisted Retention: Models and Findings," *Report of the Ninth Quadrennial Review of Military Compensation*, Vol. 3, Washington, D.C.: Office of the Undersecretary of Defense for Personnel and Readiness, 2002, Chapter 2.

Golding, Heide L. W., Jeremy A. Arkes, and Martha E. Koopman, *Compensating the Sailor of the Future*, Alexandria, Va.: Center for Naval Analyses, CRM 99-58, 1999.

Gotz, Glenn A., and John Joseph McCall, *A Dynamic Retention Model for Air Force Officers: Theory and Estimates*, Santa Monica, Calif.: RAND Corporation, R-3028-AF, 1984.

Gotz, Glenn A., and Richard Stanton, *Modeling the Contribution of Maintenance Manpower to Readiness and Sustainability*, Santa Monica, Calif.: RAND Corporation, R-3200-FMP, 1986.

Greenwood, Jeremy, and Mehmet Yorukoglu, "1974," *Carnegie-Rochester Conference Series on Public Policy*, Vol. 46, No. 1997, pp. 49–95.

Hogan, Vincent, and Roberto Rigoban, *Using Heteroscedasticity to Estimate the Returns to Education*, Cambridge, Mass.: National Bureau of Economic Research, NBER Working Paper No. 9145, September 2002.

Hosek, James R., and Michael G. Mattock, *Learning About Quality: How the Quality of Military Personnel Is Revealed over Time*, Santa Monica, Calif.: RAND Corporation, MR-1593-OSD, 2003.

Hosek, James R., and Mark Totten, *Does Perstempo Hurt Reenlistment? The Effect of Long or Hostile Perstempo on Reenlistment*, Santa Monica, Calif.: RAND Corporation, MR-990-OSD, 1998.

Hosek, James R., and Mark Totten, *Serving Away from Home: How Deployments Influence Reenlistment*, Santa Monica, Calif.: RAND Corporation, MR-1594-OSD, 2002.

Ifo Institute for Economic Research, "Growth and Productivity," in *Report on the European Economy 2002*, Munich, Germany: European Economic Advisory Group at CES ifo, 2002, Chapter 5, pp. 57–70.

Information Technology Association of America (ITAA), *Help Wanted: The IT Workforce Gap at the Dawn of a New Century*, Arlington, Va., 1997.

Information Technology Association of America (ITAA), *Help Wanted 1998: A Call for Collaborative Action for the New Millennium*, Arlington, Va., 1998.

Information Technology Association of America (ITAA), *When Can You Start? Building Better Information Technology Skills and Careers*, April 2001, www.itaa.org/workforce/studies/01execsumm.htm, last accessed May 1, 2003.

InformationWeek, homepage, www.informationweek.com/career/default.html, last accessed May 1, 2003.

"Israeli Army Computer Corps Builds Success in Business," *The New York Times*, July 24, 1999, p. B2.

Jacobs, Paula, "IT: Trade or Profession? Perception of Field Changes as Business Skills Become Critical," *InfoWorld*, Vol. 20, No. 26, June 29, 1998, pp. 113–114.

Jaeger, David A., *Estimating the Returns to Education Using the Newest Current Population Survey Education Questions*, Bonn, Germany: Institute for the Study of Labor (IZA), Discussion Paper Number 500, May 2002.

"Job-Hopping No Longer a Black Mark," *Office Systems*, November 1, 1998, p. 8.

JobSmart, homepage, www.jobsmart.org, last accessed May 1, 2003.

Jorgenson, Dale W., "Information Technology and the U.S. Economy," *American Economic Review*, Vol. 91, No. 1, March 2001, pp. 1–32.

Junor, L., and J. Oi, *A New Approach to Modeling Ship Readiness*, Alexandria, Va.: Center for Naval Analyses, CRM 95-239, 1996

Keane, Michael P., and Kenneth I. Wolpin, "The Career Decisions of Young Men," *Journal of Political Economy*, Vol. 105, No. 3, 1997, pp. 473–522.

Kelley, Colleen, President of the National Treasury Employees Union, testimony before the House Subcommittee on Technology and Procurement Policy Government Reform, U.S. House of Representatives, October 2001, http://reform.house.gov/tapps/hearings/10-4-01/NTEU.htm, last accessed May 1, 2003.

Kilburn, M. Rebecca, and Beth J. Asch, eds., *Recruiting Youth in the College Market: Current Practices and Future Policy Options*, Santa Monica, Calif.: RAND Corporation, MR-1093-OSD, 2003.

Lerman, Robert I., "Emerging Trends in the Information Technology Job Market: How Should the Public Sectors Respond?" testimony before the House Committee on Education and the Workforce, Subcommittee on Oversight and Investigations, Washington, D.C.: Urban Institute, April 1998, http://urban.org/url.cfm?ID=6930, last accessed May 1, 2003.

Lillard, Lee A., and M. Rebecca Kilburn, unpublished RAND Corporation research on ability and sequential schooling choices: instruments, siblings, and a natural experiment.

Mansell-Lewis, Emma, "Get Ready to Stress," *Computer Weekly*, April 9, 1998, p. S12.

McClure, David L., "Attracting and Retaining a High-Quality Information Technology Workforce," testimony before the Subcommittee on Technology and Procurement Policy Committee on Government Reform, U.S. House of Representatives, General Accounting Office, October 2001, http://web.archive.org/web/20021219001609/http://reform.house.gov/tapps/hearings/10-4-01/GAO.htm, last accessed December 2003.

McHugh, Jane, "Information Technology Provides Career Gateway for Some Enlisted," *Army Times*, May 25, 1998, p. 6.

"Measuring the CPI," *Journal of Economic Perspectives*, Vol. 12, No. 1, pp. 3–78, http://links.jstor.org/sici?sici=0895-3309%28199824%2912%3A1%3C%3E1.0.CO%3B2-R, last accessed May 1, 2003.

Microsoft Certified Professional, homepage, www.microsoft.com, last accessed May 1, 2003.

National Academy of Public Administration (NAPA), *The Transforming Power of Information: Making the Federal Government an Employer of Choice for IT Employees*, Washington, D.C., 2001.

National Research Council, *Computing Professionals—Changing Needs for the 1990s*, Washington, D.C.: National Academy Press, 1993.

Orvis, Bruce, Michael Childress, and J. Michael Polich, *Effect of Personnel Quality on the Performance of Patriot Air Defense System Operators*, Santa Monica, Calif.: RAND Corporation, R-3901-A, 1992.

Polich, J. Michael, James N. Dertouzos, and S. James Press, *The Enlistment Bonus Experiment*, Santa Monica, Calif.: RAND Corporation, R-3353-FMP, 1986.

"Recent Restructuring Puts Signal Corps in Good Health," *Army Times*, May 18, 1998, p. 13.

Reece, Col. Ralph (Lieutenant Colonel), James Holt, and Jong Trotter, "The Future Force—A Reasoned Approach to Change," *Field Artillery*, December 1993, pp. 17–18.

Resources for Computer Professionals, www.realrates.com, last accessed May 1, 2003.

Robbert, Al, John Ausink, Jerry Ball, Tom Manacapilli, Georges Vernez, and Nancy Weaver, unpublished RAND Corporation research on determining course content for Air Force enlisted initial skill training.

Scribner, B., D. Smith, R. Baldwin, and R. Phillips, "Are Smarter Tankers Better: AFQT and Military Productivity," *Armed Forces and Society*, Vol. 12, 1986, pp. 194–206.

Shogren, Elizabeth, "U.S. Tries to Plug Computer Worker Drain," *Los Angeles Times*, November 23, 1999, pp. A1, A15.

Silvestri, George T., "Occupational Employment Projections to 2006," *Monthly Labor Review*, Vol. 120, No. 11, November 1997, pp. 58–83.

Solow, Robert M., "We'd Better Watch Out," *New York Review of Books*, Vol. 91, No. 1, July 12, 1987, p. 36.

Stewart, Kenneth J., and Stephen B. Reed, "CPI Research Series Using Current Methods, 1978–98," *Monthly Labor Review*, Vol. 122, No. 6, June 1999, pp. 29–38.

Tice, Jim, "Automated Logistical Specialists 'The Backbone of Army Readiness,'" *Army Times*, March 30, 1998, p. 6.

Upson, Donald, remarks before the Subcommittee on Technology and Procurement Committee on Government Reform, U.S. House of Representatives, October 2001, http://web.archive.org/web/20030309122145/http://reform.house.gov/tapps/hearings/10-4-01/Upson.htm, last accessed December 2003.

U.S. Army Personnel Command, (PERSCOM), *CMF 74 Review*, April 3, 2001.

U.S. Department of Commerce, "Go for IT," www.ta.doc.gov/go4it/, last accessed May 1, 2003.

U.S. Department of Commerce, Office of Technology Policy, *America's New Deficit: The Shortage of Information Technology Workers*, 1997.

U.S. Department of Labor in the 21st Century, www.dol.gov, last accessed May 1, 2003.

U.S. General Accounting Office, *Information Technology: Assessment of the Department of Commerce's Report on Workforce Demand and Supply*, Washington, D.C., GAO/HEHS-98-159R, 1998.

U.S. General Accounting Office, *Information Technology Management: Coast Guard Practices Can Be Improved*, GA0-01-190, December 2000, pp. 65–69, www.globalsecurity.org/security/library/report/gao/gao-01-190.htm, last accessed May 1, 2003.

U.S. Office of the Secretary of Defense, *Information Assurance and Information Technology: Training, Certification, and Personnel Management in the Department of Defense, Information Assurance and Information Technology Human Resources Integrated Process Team*, Final Report, August 27, 1999, pp. E-6, E-7.

Veterans Benefits Administration, *The Montgomery GI Bill-Active Duty*, Washington, D.C., www.gibill.va.gov/education/c30pam.htm#_Toc518285755 last accessed May 1, 2003.

Vincent, Lynn, "Microsoft Targets Military for Info Technology Careers," *Army Times*, February 1, 1999, p. R7.

Warner, John, Curtis Simon, and Deborah Payne, *Enlistment Supply in the 1990's: A Study of the Navy College Fund and Other Enlistment Incentive Programs*, Arlington, Va.: Defense Manpower Data Center, Joint Advertising and Market Research Division, Report Number 2000-15, April 2001.

"What You Need to Know About: U.S. Military," www.usmilitary.about.com/library/weekly/aa092500a.htm, last accessed May 1, 2003.

Winkler, John, and J. Michael Polich, *Effectiveness of Interactive Videodisc in Army Communications Training*, Santa Monica, Calif.: RAND Corporation, R-3848-FMP, 1990.

Winstead, Donald J., Acting Associate Director for Workforce Compensation and Performance, Office of Personnel Management, testimony before the Subcommittee on Technology and Procurement Policy Committee on Government Reform, U.S. House of Representatives, October 2001, http://web.archive.org/web/20030309122132/http://reform.house.gov/tapps/hearings/10-4-01/OPM.htm, last accessed December 2003.

Zingalie, Jennifer, "Destroyers, a Century of Greatness," *Navy Newsstand: The Source for Navy News*, November 27, 2002, www.news.navy.mil/search/display.asp?story_id=4804, last accessed May 1, 2003.